W9-AZY-037

# Macmillan

# SPELLING

Senior Author
**Carl B. Smith**

Author
**Barbara Elder Weller**

**Macmillan Publishing Company**
New York

**Collier Macmillan Publishers**
London

**Copyright © 1987, 1983 Macmillan Publishing Company, a division of Macmillan, Inc.**

All rights reserved. No part of this book (except pages 25, 49, 73, 97, 121, and 145) may be reproduced or transmitted in any form or by any means, electronic or mechanical, including photocopying, recording, or by any information storage and retrieval system, without permission in writing from the Publisher.

The handwriting models in this book are reproduced with the permission of Zaner-Bloser, Inc., from the series *Creative Growth with Handwriting,* © 1979.

The contents of the Spelling Dictionary entries in this book have been adapted from *The Macmillan Beginning Dictionary,* © 1987 by Macmillan Publishing Company, a division of Macmillan, Inc.

**Cover Credit:** Photography, Bob Emmott/*Mueller & Wister Studio.*

**Illustration Credits:** Jean Gardner, Fred Harsh, Verlin Miller, Bill Ogden, Hima Pamoedjo.

**Photography Credits:** © Clara Aich. *Black Star:* © Theodore Paige. © *Colour Library International.* © Dr. E.R. Degginger, FPSA. *Leo de Wys, Inc.:* © E. Bordis, © E.C. Johnson, © B. Kaufman, © Y. Momatiuk. © Michal Heron. © Thomas Ives. *Monkmeyer Press Photo:* © Freda Leinwand. *Photo Researchers, Inc.:* © Bill Belknap, © Van Bucher, © Allen Green, © Farrell Grehan, © Jan Halaska, © Russ Kinne, © Michael P. Mannheim, © Will McIntyre, © R. Rowan, © Sarval. *Shostal Associates:* © Maury Englander, © Tom Jones, © Tom M. Morton, © W. O'Brien, © August Upitis. *Tom Stack & Associates:* © Red Planck. *Stock Boston, Inc.:* © Philip J. Bailey, © Mike Mazzaschi, © Gary Wolinsky. © Joseph F. Viesti.

Macmillan Publishing Company, a division of Macmillan, Inc.
866 Third Avenue, New York, New York 10022
Collier Macmillan Canada, Inc.
Printed in the United States of America
ISBN 0-02-287490-9
9 8 7 6 5 4

# TABLE OF CONTENTS

# HOW TO STUDY SPELLING WORDS

# TABLE OF ENGLISH SPELLINGS

This table shows the different ways that sounds may be spelled in English. For each sound, the spellings are listed in the order they most frequently appear in words. Use the table to help you locate words that you know how to pronounce but don't know how to spell.

| Sound | Spelling | Sound | Spelling |
|-------|----------|-------|----------|
| /a/ | hand, have, laugh, plaid | /o/ | lock, watch |
| /ā/ | paper, rate, rain, pay, eight, steak, veil, obey, ballet, straight, gauge | /ō/ | so, bone, boat, know, soul, foe, beau, oh, mauve, sew |
| /ä/ | father | /ô/ | off, fall, author, jaw, bought, caught, broad |
| /är/ | car, heart, sergeant | /oi/ | foil, toy |
| /ãr/ | dare, hair, where, pear, their, prayer | /ôr/ | fork, war, ore, oar, four, door |
| /b/ | bit, rabbit | /ou/ | out, now, bough |
| /ch/ | chin, nature, batch, question, cello | /p/ | pill, happy |
| /d/ | dive, ladder, would, failed | /r/ | ray, parrot, wrong, rhyme |
| /e/ | met, bread, many, said, friend, leopard, aesthetic, says, heifer | /s/ | song, city, mess, scene, listen, psychology, waltz, sword |
| /ē/ | he, city, bee, beach, athlete, machine, field, receive, key, Caesar, amoeba, people | /sh/ | nation, shin, special, mission, expansion, machine, sugar, tissue, conscience, ocean |
| /ėr/ | fern, turn, thirst, worst, earth, courage, amateur, myrtle | /t/ | ten, bitter, topped, doubt, two, ptomaine, yacht, thyme |
| /f/ | fine, phone, off, half, laugh | /th/ | thin |
| /g/ | go, stagger, vague, guard, ghost | /u/ | sun, son, touch, come, flood, does |
| /h/ | he, whom | /u̇/ | full, look, should, wolf |
| /hw/ | wheel | /ü/ | tool, luminous, who, flute, soup, jewel, true, lose, fruit, maneuver, canoe |
| /i/ | bit, myth, give, damage, build, been, pretty, carriage, busy, women | /ū/ | music, use, few, feud, cue, view, beautiful, adieu |
| /ī/ | fine, tiger, try, high, tie, dye, eye, stein, height, buy, aisle | /v/ | vine, halve, of |
| /ir/ | clear, cheer, here, cashier, souvenir, weird | /w/ | we, queen |
| /j/ | magic, jump, ledger, graduate, adjust, exaggerate, soldier | /y/ | onion, yes |
| /k/ | cat, key, tack, chord, account, mosquito, Iraq, walk | /z/ | has, zoo, xylophone, fuzz, scissor, czar, tsar |
| /kw/ | quit | /zh/ | division, treasure, garage, azure, equation |
| /l/ | line, hall, isle | /ə/ | summon, alone, April, moment, furious, circus, oxygen, ancient, bargain, surgeon |
| /m/ | mine, hammer, climb, salmon, hymn | /ər/ | better, color, dollar, augur, picture, giraffe |
| /n/ | nice | | |
| /ng/ | sing, link, tongue | | |

1

# THE /a/ and /e/ SOUNDS

A NEW

**A NEW**

hand
spell
fast
am
end
add
spend
an
well
and

**B REVIEW**

dad
has
bad
at
had

**C CHALLENGE**

shall
napkin
as
help
wagon

/**a**/ is spelled **a** as in *cat*
/**e**/ is spelled **e** as in *bed*

Read the words. Listen for the sounds of /**a**/ and /**e**/.
Then write the words.

1. Which words begin with the /**a**/ sound? Underline
   the endings of the **New** words.   am

2. Which words have the /**a**/ sound in the middle?

3. Which word begins with the /**e**/ sound?

4. Which words have the /**e**/ sound in the middle?
   Underline the **New** word that means "fine."

**■■■■■■ HANDWRITING MODELS ■■■■■■**

| • *hand* | *add* | • *dad* | • *shall* |
| *spell* | *spend* | *has* | *napkin* |
| *fast* | *an* | *bad* | *as* |
| *am* | *well* | *at* | *help* |
| *end* | *and* | *had* | *wagon* |

# Practice

**A** Write the **New** word to complete each sentence.

1. John can run very ____.   fast
2. Rita does not feel ____.
3. Jack ____ Ann like to sing.
4. Kim fell and hurt her ____.
5. My sister can ____ her name.

6. I have a dollar to ____.
7. I ____ nine years old.
8. He lives at the ____ of the street.
9. Jean will ____ up all the numbers.
10. Bob ate a pear and ____ apple.

**B** Name each picture. Write the **Review** word with the same beginning sound.

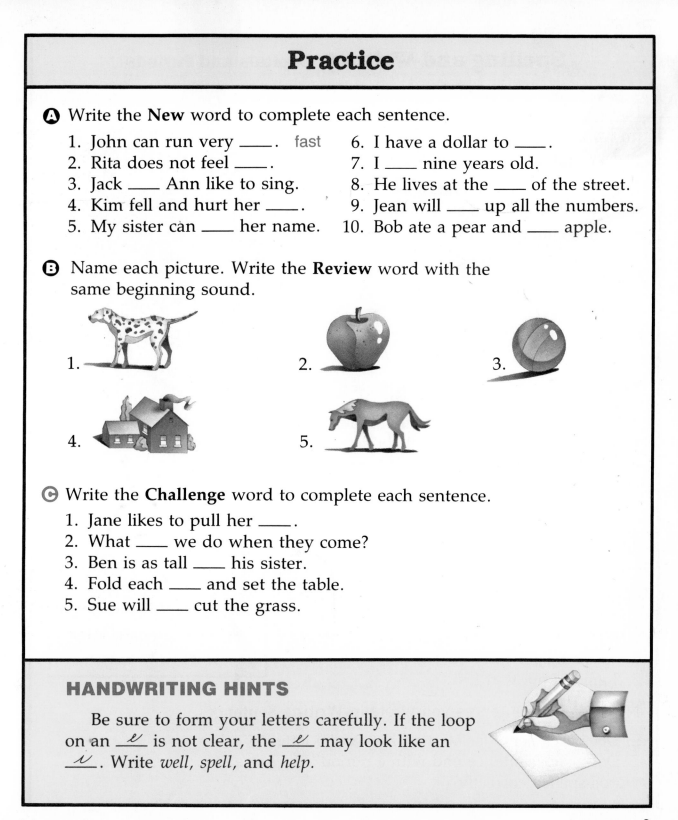

1.

2.

3.

4.

5.

**C** Write the **Challenge** word to complete each sentence.

1. Jane likes to pull her ____.
2. What ____ we do when they come?
3. Ben is as tall ____ his sister.
4. Fold each ____ and set the table.
5. Sue will ____ cut the grass.

## HANDWRITING HINTS

Be sure to form your letters carefully. If the loop on an _ℓ_ is not clear, the _ℓ_ may look like an _ι_. Write *well*, *spell*, and *help*.

# Spelling and Writing: Capitals and Periods

Use a *capital letter* to begin the first word in a sentence.

The children play outdoors.

Use a *period* (.) at the end of a sentence that makes a statement.

Three children run a race.

# Writing Sentences

Think about playing on the school playground. Write three sentences that tell about a game you play. In each sentence use one list word such as *fast, hand,* or *and*.

# Editing sentences

Use these symbols to edit the sentences. Write your edited sentences.

1. john hurt his his hand.   John hurt his hand.
2. you can spel and add.
3. I am am not that fast.

| ≡ | make a capital letter |
| ℓ | take out |

Now edit the sentences you wrote in **Writing Sentences.**

☐ Does each sentence start with a capital letter?
☐ Does each sentence end with a period?   ☐ Are all words spelled correctly?

# Review

What letters are missing? Complete each **New**, **Review**, and **Challenge** word. Write the word.

**Ⓐ**
1. h _a_ nd
2. __ m
3. __ n
4. sp __ ll
5. sp __ nd
6. f __ st
7. __ dd
8. __ nd
9. __ nd
10. w __ ll

**Ⓑ**
1. d __ d
2. h __ s
3. b __ d
4. __ t
5. h __ d

**Ⓒ**
1. sh __ ll
2. n __ pkin
3. __ s
4. w __ gon
5. h __ lp

# Word Building

**For many words, do not change the end of the word before adding *-ed* or *-ing*.**

end + ed = ended     end + ing = ending

Add the ending to each word. Write the complete word.

1. Yesterday I (help + ed) my brother.   helped
2. Today I am (help + ing) my sister.
3. I (spell + ed) a word before.
4. I am (spell + ing) a new word now.
5. You (hand + ed) me a note earlier.
6. You are (hand + ing) me a letter now.

# Content Words

You may use these /a/ and /e/ words in your math class.

**less     eleven     subtract**

Write a word to complete each sentence. Use the Spelling Dictionary in the back of your book.

1. You ____ to find how many are left.
2. Four is ____ than nine.
3. Add six and five to get ____.

/i/ is spelled **i** as in *six*
/o/ is spelled **o** as in *clock*
/ô/ is spelled **o** as in *dog*

## Ⓐ NEW

spot
swim
trip
in
doll
off
on
will
lots
it

## Ⓑ REVIEW

lot
his
him
from
is

## Ⓒ CHALLENGE

quit
across
often
minute
instead

Read the words. Listen for the sounds of /i/, /o/, and /ô/. Then write the words.

1. Which words begin with the /i/ sound? Underline the different endings of the **New** words.

2. Which words have the /i/ sound in the middle? Underline the vowel in the **New** words.

3. Which words begin with the /o/ or /ô/ sounds? Underline the endings of the **New** words.

4. Which words have the /o/ or /ô/ sound in the middle? Underline the word that means "a great amount."

### ▮ HANDWRITING MODELS ▮

- *spot*
  *swim*
  *trip*
  *in*
  *doll*

  *off*
  *on*
  *will*
  *lots*
  *it*

- *lot*
  *his*
  *him*
  *from*
  *is*

- *quit*
  *across*
  *often*
  *minute*
  *instead*

# Practice

**A** What letter is missing? Write the **New** words.

1. The cat is __n the roof.
2. I don't like __t!
3. There is a sp__t on your shirt.
4. We have l__ts to do.
5. Let's take a sw__m in the pool.
6. What w__ll Jan do now?
7. We are leaving for our tr__p.
8. Please get __ff the table!
9. Mom took it __n the house.
10. Jane has a new d__ll.

**B** Read the sentences. Write the missing **Review** words.

Sam walked home __(1)__ school. He had a __(2)__ of books. A dog ran into __(3)__. Sam fell and hurt __(4)__ foot. Now his foot __(5)__ in a cast.

**C** Finish the puzzle with **Challenge** words. Write each word.

## HANDWRITING HINTS

Be sure to form your letters carefully. If the ending loop on an _o_ comes down too far, the _o_ may look like an _a_. Write *on*, *mop*, and *top*.

# Spelling and Writing: Question and Exclamation Marks

Use a *question mark* (?) at the end of a sentence that asks something.

Where do you stay?

Use an *exclamation mark* (!) at the end of a sentence that shows strong feeling.

What an exciting place we saw!

# Writing Sentences

Think about the campsite in the picture. Write two question sentences about what the family does. Write an exclamation sentence that tells something exciting that happens. Use one list word in each sentence, such as *in*, *on*, and *swim*.

# Editing sentencess

Use these symbols to edit the sentences. Write your edited sentences.

1. did she learn to to swim?
2. what a great tripp it was!

| ☰ make a capital letter |
| take out |

Now edit the sentences you wrote in **Writing Sentences.**

☐ Does each sentence start with a capital letter?
☐ Does each sentence end with a question mark or an exclamation mark?  ☐ Are all words spelled correctly?

# Review

Write the **New, Review,** and **Challenge** words in the chart.

| | /i/ spelled **i** | | /o/ spelled **o** | /ô/ spelled **o** |
|---|---|---|---|---|
| **A** | | | | |
| | | | | |
| | | | | |
| **B** | | | | |
| | | | | |
| **C** | | | | |
| | | | | |

# Word Building

**If a word ends with consonant-vowel-consonant, double the final consonant before adding _-ed_ or _-ing_.**

   spot + ed = spotted      spot + ing = spotting

Add the ending to each word. Write the complete word.

1. Joey (stop + ed) me before.   stopped
2. Maria is (stop + ing) me now.
3. Yesterday I (plan + ed) to go.
4. Today I am (plan + ing) to stay.
5. I (hop + ed) on rocks earlier.

# Content Words

You may use these /i/, /o/, and /ô/ words in your social studies class.

   **cost      drill      monument**

Write a word to complete each sentence. Use the Spelling Dictionary for help.

1. They built a ____ to honor the man.
2. He cut holes in the rock with a ____.
3. What is the ____ of that new game?

# 3 THE /u/ and /u̇/ SOUNDS

/u/ is spelled **u** as in *pup*
/u̇/ is spelled **u** as in *push*
        **oo** as in *book*

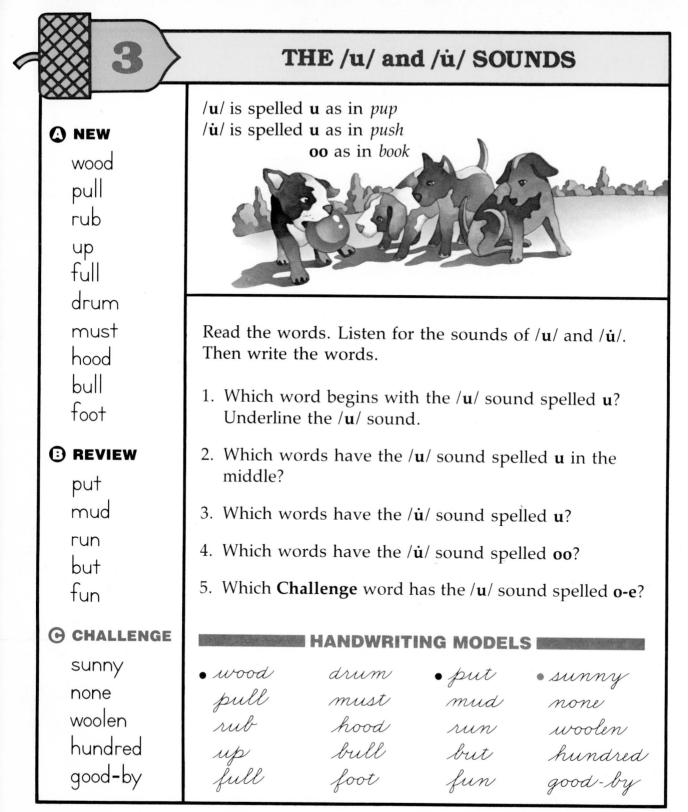

### A NEW

wood
pull
rub
up
full
drum
must
hood
bull
foot

### B REVIEW

put
mud
run
but
fun

### C CHALLENGE

sunny
none
woolen
hundred
good-by

Read the words. Listen for the sounds of /u/ and /u̇/.
Then write the words.

1. Which word begins with the /u/ sound spelled **u**?
   Underline the /u/ sound.

2. Which words have the /u/ sound spelled **u** in the
   middle?

3. Which words have the /u̇/ sound spelled **u**?

4. Which words have the /u̇/ sound spelled **oo**?

5. Which **Challenge** word has the /u/ sound spelled **o-e**?

### ▄▄▄▄ HANDWRITING MODELS ▄▄▄▄

- *wood*    *drum*
  *pull*    *must*
  *rub*    *hood*
  *up*    *bull*
  *full*    *foot*
- *put*    • *sunny*
  *mud*    *none*
  *run*    *woolen*
  *but*    *hundred*
  *fun*    *good-by*

# Practice

**A** Write the missing **New** words. Each word will rhyme with the underlined word.

The <u>bull</u> began to __(1)__ .

Don't try to <u>pull</u> the __(2)__ .

To get clean, <u>scrub</u> and __(3)__ .

The <u>cup</u> was filled __(4)__ .

The <u>soot</u> fell on his __(5)__ .

To clean and <u>dust</u> is a __(6)__ .

It <u>could</u> be made of __(7)__ .

He'll <u>hum</u> as you __(8)__ .

The bag of <u>wool</u> was __(9)__ .

You <u>should</u> wear the __(10)__ .

**B** What letter is missing? Write each **Review** word.

1. m_d
2. f_n
3. b_t
4. r_n
5. p_t

**C** Name each picture. Write the **Challenge** word with the same beginning sound.

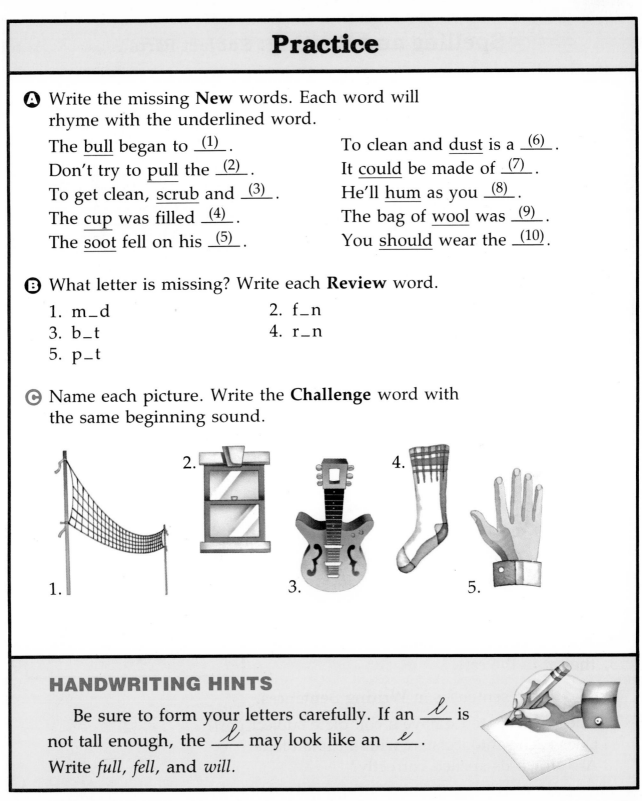

1.

2.

3.

4.

5.

## HANDWRITING HINTS

Be sure to form your letters carefully. If an _ℓ_ is not tall enough, the _ℓ_ may look like an _e_.
Write *full*, *fell*, and *will*.

A sentence has two parts. The *subject part* of a sentence names whom or what the sentence is about. The subject part may have one word or more than one word. The subject part of each of these sentences is underlined.

<u>Raúl</u> plays the drum.
<u>The children</u> march in line.

# Writing Sentences

Think about the Fourth of July parade. Write a subject part to complete each sentence. Use a list word in each, such as *drum*, *foot*, or *bull*.

1. ____ sounds loud.
2. ____ feels sore.
3. ____ pulls the cart.

# Editing sentences

Each sentence below is missing part of its subject part. Use these symbols to edit the sentences. Write your edited sentences.

1. the played in the band.   The boy played
2. A marched in the parade.   in the band.
3. the sat in the cart.

| ≡ | make a capital letter |
| ^ | add words |
| ℓ | take out |

Now edit the sentences in **Writing Sentences.**

☐ Does each sentence have a complete subject part?
☐ Does each sentence start with a capital letter?
☐ Are all words spelled correctly?

# Review

What letters are missing? Complete each **New**, **Review**, and **Challenge** word. Write the word.

**Ⓐ** 1. r_b
  2. w__d
  3. f_ll
  4. h__d
  5. b_ll
  6. _p
  7. p_ll
  8. dr_m
  9. f__t
  10. m_st

**Ⓑ** 1. m_d
  2. p_t
  3. r_n
  4. b_t
  5. f_n

**Ⓒ** 1. s_nny
  2. n_n_
  3. w__len
  4. h_ndred
  5. g__d-by

# Word Building

**Add -s to many nouns to name more than one.**

one <u>drum</u>
two <u>drums</u>

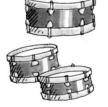

one <u>bull</u>
many <u>bulls</u>

Add -s to each word. Write the complete word.

1. I see three (doll + s).  dolls
2. They ride in two (wagon + s).
3. We set out four (napkin + s).
4. She takes many (trip + s).
5. We wait five (minute + s).
6. The tiger has many (spot + s).

# Content Words

You may use these /u/ and /u̇/ words in your science class.

**woodlands    pulley    sunset**

Write a word to complete each sentence. Use the Spelling Dictionary for help.

1. A ____ can lift heavy things.
2. Wild animals live in the ____ .
3. It grows dark at ____ .

# THE /ā/ SOUND

/ā/ is spelled **a-e** as in *gate*
**ai** as in *rain*
**ay** as in *jay*

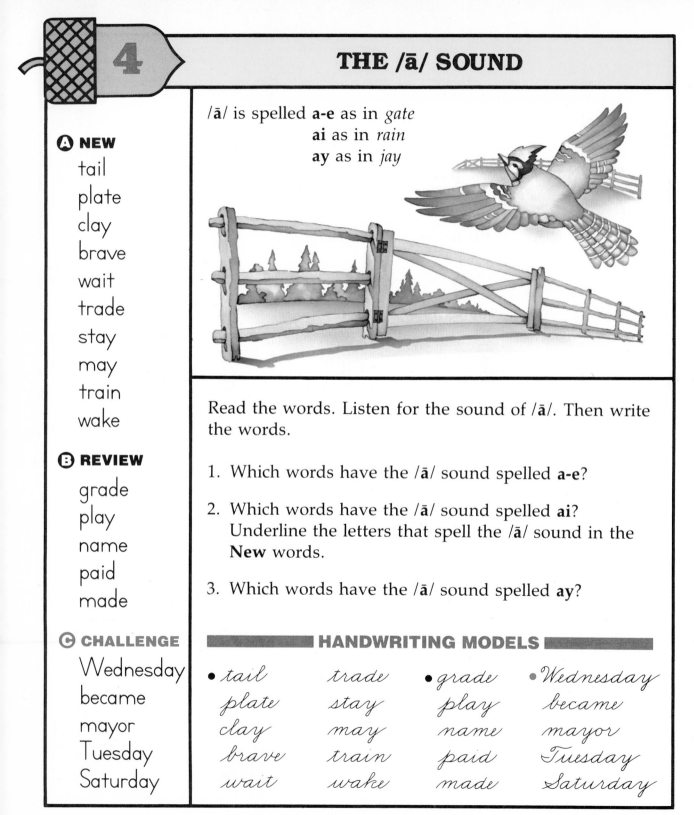

## A NEW

tail
plate
clay
brave
wait
trade
stay
may
train
wake

## B REVIEW

grade
play
name
paid
made

## C CHALLENGE

Wednesday
became
mayor
Tuesday
Saturday

Read the words. Listen for the sound of /ā/. Then write the words.

1. Which words have the /ā/ sound spelled **a-e**?

2. Which words have the /ā/ sound spelled **ai**? Underline the letters that spell the /ā/ sound in the **New** words.

3. Which words have the /ā/ sound spelled **ay**?

### HANDWRITING MODELS

- *tail*      *trade*      • *grade*      • *Wednesday*
  *plate*     *stay*       *play*        *became*
  *clay*      *may*        *name*        *mayor*
  *brave*     *train*      *paid*        *Tuesday*
  *wait*      *wake*       *made*        *Saturday*

# Practice

**Ⓐ** Choose a **New** word to complete each sentence. Then write each word.

It is better to stop and w __(1)__ .
My cat has a very short t __(2)__ .
Mom travels on the t __(3)__ .
Until you're told, you must s __(4)__ .
Please eat over your p __(5)__ .
If you like, we could t __(6)__ .
Is it time to w __(7)__ up?
In art class we made pots from c __(8)__ .
When frightened, try to be b __(9)__ .
Ask Dad to see if you m __(10)__ .

**Ⓑ** Write a **Review** word to complete each sentence.

John is his __(1)__ . He is in the third __(2)__ .
Maria __(3)__ 75 cents to __(4)__ the game.
Pam __(5)__ lemonade for all of us.

**Ⓒ** What letters are missing? Write the **Challenge** word.

1. m__or
2. bec_m_
3. Tuesd__

4. Wednesd__
5. Saturd__

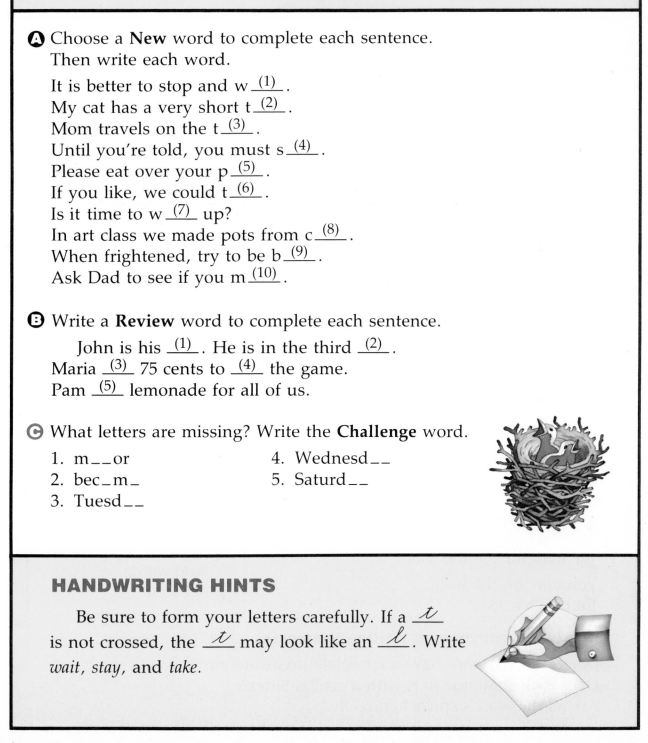

## HANDWRITING HINTS

Be sure to form your letters carefully. If a _𝓉_ is not crossed, the _𝓉_ may look like an _𝓁_ . Write *wait*, *stay*, and *take*.

# Spelling and Writing: Predicate Parts

A sentence has a subject part and a predicate part. The *predicate part* of a sentence tells what action the subject part does. The predicate part may have one word or more than one word. The predicate part of each sentence is underlined.

The train <u>arrives</u>.
The engine <u>makes a lot of noise</u>.

## Writing Sentences

Think about the old train. Write a predicate part to complete each sentence. In each sentence use a list word, such as *wait* and *play*.

1. The people ____ .
2. The two boys ____ .

## Editing sentencess

Each sentence below is missing part of its predicate part. Use these symbols to edit the sentences. Write your edited sentences.

1. the man for the the train.
2. you may on the train.
3. John to his seat.

| | |
|---|---|
| ≡ | make a capital letter |
| ∧ | add words |
| ✂ | take out |

Now edit the sentences in **Writing Sentences.**

□ Does each sentence have a complete predicate part?
□ Does each sentence start with a capital letter?
□ Are all the words spelled correctly?

# Review

Write the words that complete the chart.

| /ā/ spelled **a-e** | /ā/ spelled **ai** | /ā/ spelled **ay** |
|---|---|---|
| Ⓐ | Ⓐ | Ⓐ |
| | | |
| | | |
| | Ⓑ | Ⓑ |
| Ⓑ | | Ⓒ |
| | | |
| | | |
| Ⓒ | | |

# Dictionary Skills

Suppose you wanted to spell the /ā/ sound in . You could use the Table of English Spellings in a dictionary. It shows that the /ā/ sound may be spelled **a, a-e, ai, ay, ea,** or **ei.** In the dictionary, you would then look up the word with each possible spelling of the /ā/ sound until you found the word.

Write the correct spelling of each word.

1. skait    skate    skayt      3. payg    page    paig
2. gaym    gaim    game

# Content Words

You may use these /ā/ words in your social studies class.

    **reservation    case    plain**

Write a word to complete each sentence. Use the Spelling Dictionary for help.

1. To protect the camera put it in a ____.
2. Nearly flat or level land is a ____.
3. Some groups of people live on a ____.

# 5 THE /ē/ SOUND

/ē/ is spelled **ee** as in *beets*
**ea** as in *beans*

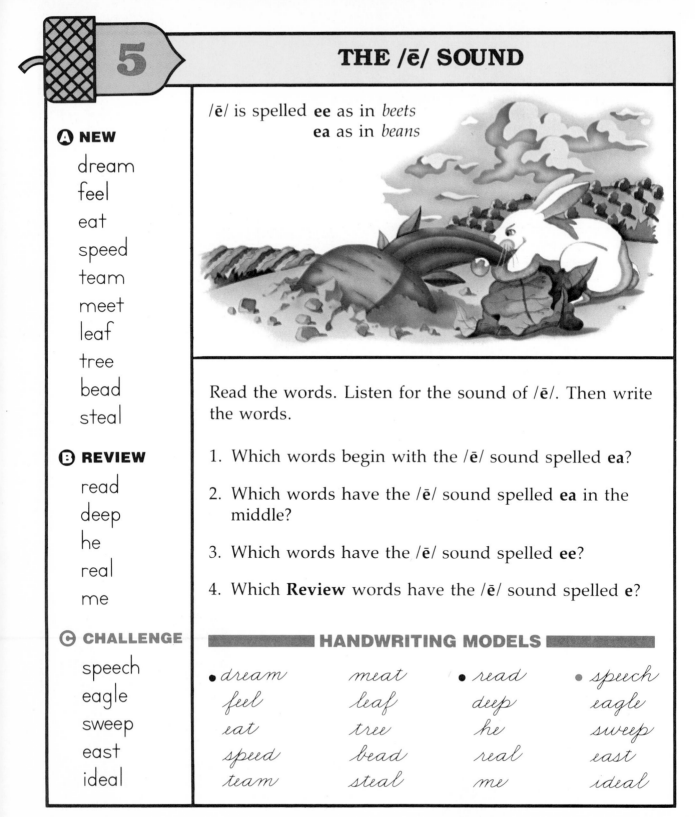

## Ⓐ NEW

dream
feel
eat
speed
team
meet
leaf
tree
bead
steal

## Ⓑ REVIEW

read
deep
he
real
me

## Ⓒ CHALLENGE

speech
eagle
sweep
east
ideal

Read the words. Listen for the sound of /ē/. Then write the words.

1. Which words begin with the /ē/ sound spelled **ea**?

2. Which words have the /ē/ sound spelled **ea** in the middle?

3. Which words have the /ē/ sound spelled **ee**?

4. Which **Review** words have the /ē/ sound spelled **e**?

### ▰▰▰ HANDWRITING MODELS ▰▰▰

- *dream*
  *feel*
  *eat*
  *speed*
  *team*

  *meat*
  *leaf*
  *tree*
  *bead*
  *steal*

- *read*
  *deep*
  *he*
  *real*
  *me*

- *speech*
  *eagle*
  *sweep*
  *east*
  *ideal*

# Practice

**A** Write the **New** word that completes each sentence.

1. Fruits and vegetables are good to ____ .
2. Carmen must string one more ____ .
3. Look at the size of that oak ____!
4. At the corner is where we'll ____ .
5. When I sleep I often ____ .
6. How do you ____?
7. Ito tried out for the baseball ____ .
8. We are going to plant a ____ .
9. Snails do not move with great ____ .
10. In the game of baseball you may ____ .

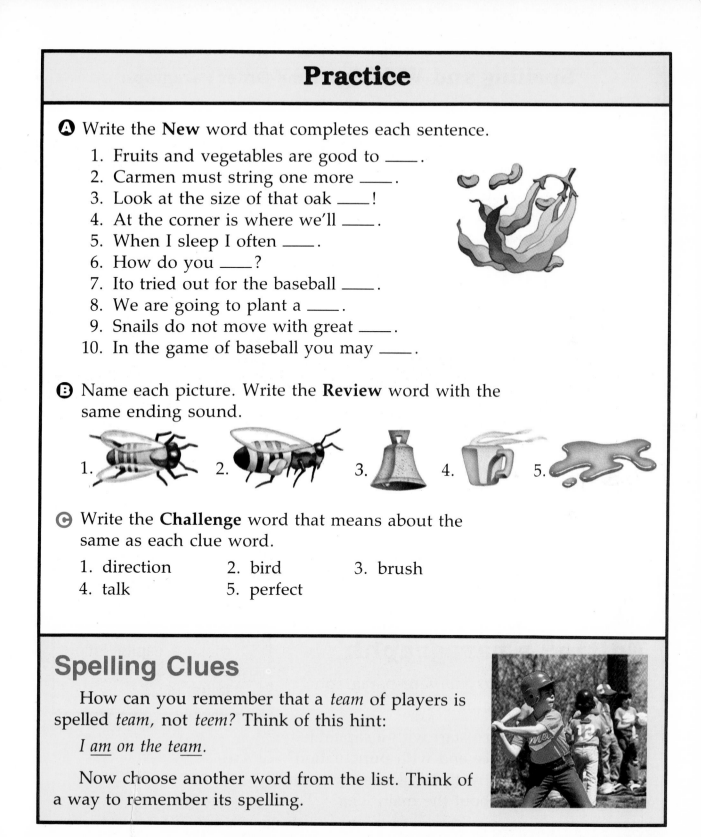

**B** Name each picture. Write the **Review** word with the same ending sound.

1. 2. 3. 4. 5.

**C** Write the **Challenge** word that means about the same as each clue word.

1. direction
2. bird
3. brush
4. talk
5. perfect

## Spelling Clues

How can you remember that a *team* of players is spelled *team*, not *teem*? Think of this hint:

*I am on the team.*

Now choose another word from the list. Think of a way to remember its spelling.

# Spelling and Writing: Time-Order Paragraph

A *paragraph* is a group of sentences that tells about one main idea. The *main idea sentence* states the most important idea of the paragraph. The *detail sentences* tell more about the main idea. Read this time-order paragraph. The detail sentences tell the order that something happens.

Two birds build a nest. First they find a leafy tree. Next they get sticks and string. Last they put the sticks and string together.

The first sentence in the paragraph is the main idea sentence. The other sentences are detail sentences. Words like *first*, *next*, and *last* help explain the order that things happen. Notice that the first sentence is indented.

## Writing a Paragraph

Look at the pictures. Then write a time-order paragraph that tells about the pictures. First write this main idea sentence: *The boys have fun.* Then write one detail sentence about each picture. Use at least three list words, such as *meet*, *team*, or *eat*.

## Editing a paragraph

Use these symbols to edit your paragraph. Write your edited paragraph.

☰ make a capital letter
∧ add words
℘ take out

☐ Does each sentence start with a capital letter?
☐ Does each sentence end with punctuation?  ☐ Are all words spelled correctly? ☐ Does each detail sentence tell more about the main idea?

# Review

What letters are missing? Complete each **New**, **Review**, and **Challenge** word. Write the word.

**Ⓐ**
1. st__l
2. dr__m
3. tr__
4. __t
5. sp__d
6. b__d
7. f__l
8. l__f
9. m__t
10. t__m

**Ⓑ**
1. m_
2. r__d
3. d__p
4. h_
5. r__l

**Ⓒ**
1. id__l
2. sp__ch
3. __gle
4. sw__p
5. __st

# Word Building

**Add *-y* or *-er* to the end of some words to form a new word.**

dream + y = dreamy     dream + er = dreamer

Add the ending to each word. Write the complete word.

1. I sat under the (leaf + y) tree.   leafy
2. My dog is a good (eat + er).
3. He smelled the (steam + y) vegetables.
4. That story is in my (read + er).
5. The baby looked very (sleep + y).
6. The (sweep + er) cleaned the room.

# Content Words

You may use these /ē/ words in your science class.

**heat     seashore     weed**

Write a word to complete each sentence. Use the Spelling Dictionary for help.

1. High temperature or warmth is ____.
2. An unwanted plant is a ____.
3. Land near the sea is the ____.

# UNIT 6    REVIEW: UNITS 1-5

## UNIT 1

/a/ is spelled **a**; /e/ is spelled **e**

| | | | | |
|---|---|---|---|---|
| hand | spell | fast | am | end |
| add | spend | an | well | and |

Say each word. Write each word that rhymes.

1. jam
2. can
3. mad
4. last
5. land

6. band
7. send
8. bend
9. tell
10. sell

## UNIT 2

/i/ is spelled **i**; /o/ or /ô/ are spelled **o**

| | | | | |
|---|---|---|---|---|
| spot | doll | in | off | will |
| swim | trip | on | lots | it |

Find each word in the puzzle. The words will be →
or ↓ .

Write each /i/ word.
Write each /o/ or /ô/ word.

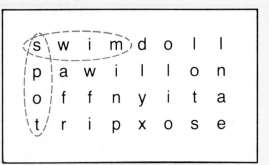

/ů/ may be spelled **oo** or **u**; /u/ may be spelled **u**

| wood | drum | rub | up | must |
| hood | full | foot | pull | bull |

Read each sentence. Write a word that means about the same as the underlined word or words.

1. Kim likes to <u>tap</u> on the table.
2. <u>Tug</u> the rope to ring the bell.
3. It has a cut on its <u>paw</u>.
4. The desk is made of <u>pine</u>.
5. The <u>cow</u> is in the field.
6. Dan had to <u>scrub</u> to get it shiny.
7. Bob and Jane <u>have to</u> study.
8. Mike climbed <u>toward</u> the top.
9. Jim ate until he was <u>stuffed</u>.
10. Pam's cape has a <u>hat</u>.

/ā/ may be spelled **a-e**, **ai**, or **ay**

| tail | plate | train | clay | brave |
| wait | stay | may | trade | wake |

Write the words that rhyme with each word.

1. they
2. great
3. sale
4. paid
5. plane
6. cave
7. make
8. play
9. weigh
10. eight

/ē/ is spelled **ee** or **ea**

| | | | | |
|---|---|---|---|---|
| dream | feel | speed | eat | meet |
| team | leaf | tree | bead | steal |

Read each clue. Finish each word in the puzzle. Write
each word.

**Across**

3. to take what is not yours
6. woody plant
9. to think when asleep
10. to think or have an opinion

**Down**

1. what mouths do
2. tells how fast
4. group of players
5. green part of a tree
7. to see someone somewhere
8. round thing on a string

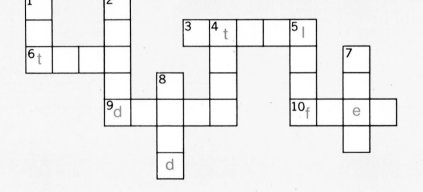

# Word Building

Add the ending to each word. Then write the new
word.

1. feel + ing =
2. pull + s =
3. eat + er =
4. trip + ed =
5. end + ed =

6. spell + ed =
7. speed + y =
8. swim + ing =
9. plate + s =
10. steam + er =

Read each sentence. If the underlined word is right, mark **Right** as your answer. If the underlined word is wrong, mark **Wrong** as your answer.

1. Maria <u>an</u> Rita can go.
   Right ⓐ   Wrong ⬤

2. The cat is <u>on</u> the roof.
   Right ⓐ   Wrong ⓑ

3. Kathy is <u>in</u> the house.
   Right ⓐ   Wrong ⓑ

4. Mike gave <u>it</u> to me.
   Right ⓐ   Wrong ⓑ

5. My cat has a long <u>tale</u>.
   Right ⓐ   Wrong ⓑ

6. I don't feel <u>well</u>.
   Right ⓐ   Wrong ⓑ

7. Pam ate <u>and</u> apple.
   Right ⓐ   Wrong ⓑ

8. I <u>em</u> 9 years old.
   Right ⓐ   Wrong ⓑ

9. When <u>will</u> he come?
   Right ⓐ   Wrong ⓑ

10. Please turn <u>of</u> the lights.
   Right ⓐ   Wrong ⓑ

Read each pair of words. Mark the word that is spelled correctly.

11. hand ⬤
    woud ⓑ

12. spot ⓐ
    dreem ⓑ

13. spel ⓐ
    feel ⓑ

14. plate ⓐ
    swin ⓑ

15. tripp ⓐ
    pull ⓑ

16. fast ⓐ
    claye ⓑ

17. eet ⓐ
    rub ⓑ

18. up ⓐ
    spead ⓑ

19. brave ⓐ
    dol ⓑ

20. ind ⓐ
    full ⓑ

21. wait ⓐ
    teme ⓑ

22. mete ⓐ
    add ⓑ

23. drum ⓐ
    traid ⓑ

24. spnd ⓐ
    must ⓑ

25. leef ⓐ
    stay ⓑ

26. hood ⓐ
    trane ⓑ

27. trea ⓐ
    may ⓑ

28. lots ⓐ
    beed ⓑ

29. steele ⓐ
    bull ⓑ

30. fut ⓐ
    wake ⓑ

# THE /ī/ SOUND

/ī/ is spelled **i-e** as in *lime*
                **i** as in *rind*
                **y** as in *fly*
                **igh** as in *light*

**Ⓐ NEW**

I
mile
drive
blind
flight
bright
dry
high
try
find

**Ⓑ REVIEW**

right
time
by
fine
my

**Ⓒ CHALLENGE**

surprise
tonight
entire
decide
pirate

Read the words. Listen for the sound of /ī/. Then write the words.

1. Which word spells the /ī/ sound? Notice that it is always capitalized.

2. Which words have the /ī/ sound spelled **i-e**?

3. Which words have the /ī/ sound spelled **i**?

4. Which words end with the /ī/ sound spelled **y**? Underline the **New** words that end in **y**.

5. Which words have the /ī/ sound spelled **igh**?

<hr>

**HANDWRITING MODELS**

| • *I* | *bright* | • *right* | • *surprise* |
|---|---|---|---|
| *mile* | *dry* | *time* | *tonight* |
| *drive* | *high* | *by* | *entire* |
| *blind* | *try* | *fine* | *decide* |
| *flight* | *find* | *my* | *pirate* |

# Practice

**A** Write the **New** word that best completes each
sentence.

   1. Let's look to see if we can ____ it.
   2. Ben lives ____ up in the mountains.
   3. Sam uses a cane because he is ____.
   4. The land is hot and ____.
   5. I will ____ to do it better.
   6. Instead of walking, we'll ____.
   7. We'll fly on the last ____ out.
   8. My sister and ____ are going.
   9. I ran half a ____ yesterday.
  10. Yellow is a ____ color.

**B** What letters are missing? Write the **Review** word.

   1. m_            4. t_m_
   2. f_n_         5. b_
   3. r___t

**C** Read each clue. Write a **Challenge** word that means the
same thing as each clue.

   1. whole         4. this evening
   2. choose       5. amaze
   3. sailor

## HANDWRITING HINTS

    Be sure to form your letters carefully. If the _i_ is
too tall, the _i_ may look like an _l_. Write *mile, pile*
and *blind*.

# Spelling and Writing: The Five Senses

You can describe a thing in five ways. You can tell how it looks, sounds, smells, tastes, or feels. Read each sentence. Notice the way something is described.

The silvery moon <u>looks</u> bright.
We step on a leaf that <u>sounds</u> crispy.
The milk I got <u>smells</u> sour.
The bread that I have <u>tastes</u> dry.
The snow on the mountain <u>feels</u> cold.

# Writing Sentences

Write three sentences that describe things in your home. In each sentence, tell how one thing looks, sounds, smells, tastes, or feels. In each sentence, use at least one list word, such as *bright, dry,* or *high.*

# Editing sentences

Add a word to each sentence to describe something. Use the symbols to edit the sentences. Write your edited sentences.

1. the high airplane sounds.
2. the dry mud looks.

| ∧ | add words |
| ≡ | make a capital letter |

Now edit the sentences you wrote in **Writing Sentences.**

☐ Does each sentence tell how something looks, sounds, smells, tastes, or feels? ☐ Are all words spelled correctly? ☐ Does each sentence start with a capital letter? ☐ Does each sentence end with a period?

# Review

Write the words that complete the chart.

| /ī/ spelled **i-e** | /ī/ spelled **i** | /ī/ spelled **y** | /ī/ spelled **igh** |
|---|---|---|---|
| Ⓐ | Ⓐ | Ⓐ | Ⓐ |
| | | | |
| Ⓑ | | | |
| | Ⓒ | | Ⓑ |
| Ⓒ | | | Ⓒ |
| | | | |
| | | | |

# Word Building

**If a word ends with a consonant and _y_, change _y_ to _i_ before adding _-es_ or _-ed_.**

try + es = tries     try + ed = tried

Add the ending to each word. Write the complete word.

1. Bob (dry + es) the dishes now.   dries
2. Pam (dry + ed) the dishes yesterday.
3. The baby (cry + es) often.
4. The baby (cry + ed) before.
5. Mother (fry + es) fish for us.
6. Father (fry + ed) fish last week.

# Content Words

You may use these /ī/ words in your math class.

**divide     multiply     size**

Write the word to complete each sentence. Use the Spelling Dictionary for help.

1. A fast way to add is to ____.
2. The bigness of something is its ____.
3. To find how many times a number goes into another you ____.

# THE /ō/ SOUND

/ō/ is spelled **o** as in *comb*
                 **o-e** as in *rose*
                 **oa** as in *throat*
                 **ow** as in *bow*

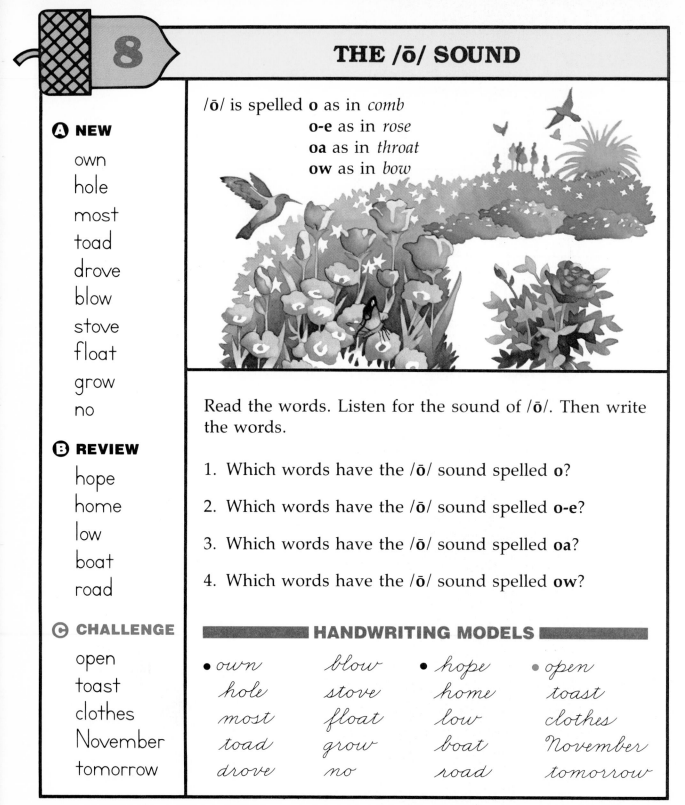

**A NEW**

own
hole
most
toad
drove
blow
stove
float
grow
no

**B REVIEW**

hope
home
low
boat
road

**C CHALLENGE**

open
toast
clothes
November
tomorrow

Read the words. Listen for the sound of /ō/. Then write the words.

1. Which words have the /ō/ sound spelled **o**?

2. Which words have the /ō/ sound spelled **o-e**?

3. Which words have the /ō/ sound spelled **oa**?

4. Which words have the /ō/ sound spelled **ow**?

**HANDWRITING MODELS**

- *own*
  *hole*
  *most*
  *toad*
  *drove*

*blow*
*stove*
*float*
*grow*
*no*

- *hope*
  *home*
  *low*
  *boat*
  *road*

- *open*
  *toast*
  *clothes*
  *November*
  *tomorrow*

# Practice

**Ⓐ** What letters are missing? Write the **New** word.

1. The plants will gr__.
2. We dr_v_ home early.
3. My boat won't fl__t.
4. There is a t__d by the road.
5. I have my __n bike.

6. There is a h_l_ in it.
7. Bl__ out all the candles.
8. There are n_ more left.
9. Maria has the m_st crayons.
10. Hot soup is on the st_v_.

**Ⓑ** Name each picture. Write the **Review** word with the same ending sound.

1.     2.     3.

4.     5.

**Ⓒ** Read the clues. Write a **Challenge** word for each. The word in the box gives the answer to this riddle.

**Riddle**: What is a pole that no one can climb?

1. unwrap          _ _ _|_|_
2. a month         _|_|_ _ _ _ _
3. after today     _ _ _ _|_|_ _ _
4. browned bread   _|_|_ _ _
5. dresses and shoes _ _ _ _|_|_ _

## HANDWRITING HINTS

Be sure to form your letters carefully.
If a  is not left open at the top, the _v_ may look like an _o_. Write *stove*, *drove*, and *love*.

# Spelling and Writing: Verbs

A *verb* is a word that names an action. When you write sentences, you should always use the best verb to tell about the action. The verb in each of these sentences is underlined.

The children <u>have</u> hats.
The children <u>wear</u> hats.

The verbs *have* and *wear* mean almost the same thing. But *wear* more closely names the action.

# Writing Sentences

Think about the children's party. Write two sentences that tell about the actions. Use a good verb from the list, such as *blow*, *float*, *grow*, *drove*, or *own*.

# Editing sentencess

Replace the underlined verb with a verb that most closely names the action. Use the symbols to edit the sentences. Write your edited sentences.

| ^ | add words |
|---|---|
| ℘ | take out |

1. I <u>have</u> my own record.

2. The children <u>walk</u> to the music.

Now edit the sentences you wrote in **Writing Sentences.**

☐ Does each sentence have the best verb? ☐ Are all words spelled correctly?

# Review

What letters are missing? Complete each **New**, **Review**, and **Challenge** word. Write the word.

**A** 1. n_
2. gr__
3. fl__t
4. st_v_
5. t__d

6. __n
7. h_l_
8. m_st
9. bl__
10. dr_v_

**B** 1. r__d
2. l__
3. h_p_
4. b__t
5. h_m_

**C** 1. cl_th_s
2. N_vember
3. tomorr__
4. _pen
5. t__st

# Word Building

**If a word ends with a consonant and _-e_, drop the _-e_ before adding _-ing_ or _-ed_.**

close + ing = closing     close + ed = closed

Add the ending to each word. Write the complete word.

1. The dog is (chase + ing) a rabbit now.   chasing
2. The rabbit (chase + ed) the dog earlier.
3. Boys are (trade + ing) baseball cards.
4. The girls (trade + ed) cards with them.
5. A clown is (joke + ing) with the child.
6. The clown (joke + ed) with me before.

# Content Words

You may use these /ō/ words in your social studies class.

**coast     arrow     sold**

Write a word to complete each sentence. Use the Spelling Dictionary for help.

1. A boat can sail along the ____.
2. An ____ is used with a bow.
3. Things can be bought and ____ in a store.

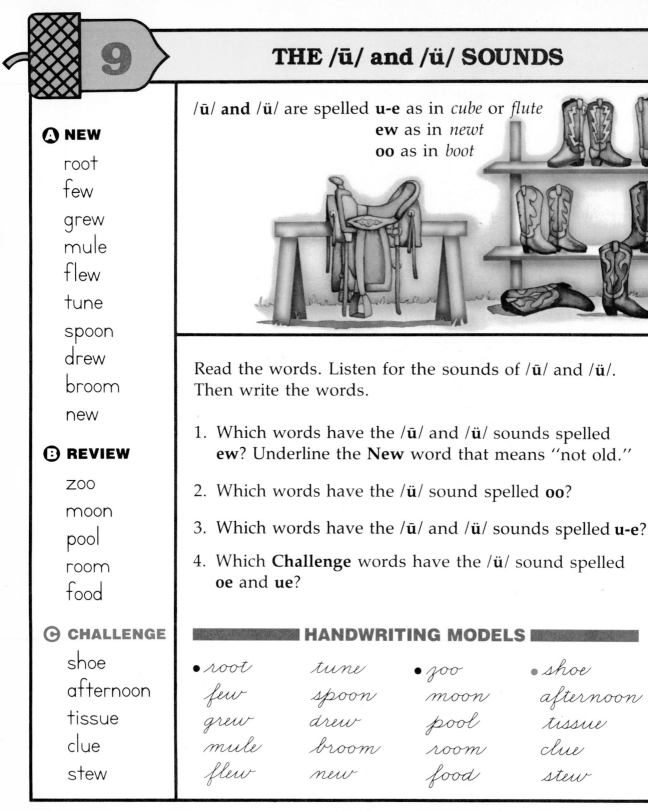

# 9 · THE /ū/ and /ü/ SOUNDS

## Ⓐ NEW

root
few
grew
mule
flew
tune
spoon
drew
broom
new

## Ⓑ REVIEW

zoo
moon
pool
room
food

## Ⓒ CHALLENGE

shoe
afternoon
tissue
clue
stew

/ū/ and /ü/ are spelled **u-e** as in *cube* or *flute*
**ew** as in *newt*
**oo** as in *boot*

Read the words. Listen for the sounds of /ū/ and /ü/.
Then write the words.

1. Which words have the /ū/ and /ü/ sounds spelled
   **ew**? Underline the **New** word that means "not old."

2. Which words have the /ü/ sound spelled **oo**?

3. Which words have the /ū/ and /ü/ sounds spelled **u-e**?

4. Which **Challenge** words have the /ü/ sound spelled
   **oe** and **ue**?

### ▰▰▰ HANDWRITING MODELS ▰▰▰

| • root | tune | • zoo | • shoe |
| few | spoon | moon | afternoon |
| grew | drew | pool | tissue |
| mule | broom | room | clue |
| flew | new | food | stew |

34 *Develop*

# Practice

**A** What letters are missing? Write the **New** word.

1. My dress is n_ _.
2. The r_ _t grows underground.
3. I'll sweep it with a br_ _m.
4. He has very f_ _ pieces left.
5. My brother gr_ _ two inches.

6. Maria dr_ _ the picture.
7. Ed played a t_n_ on the piano.
8. The m_l_ pulled the cart.
9. The bird fl_ _ away.
10. Eat your soup with a sp_ _n!

**B** Name each picture. Write the **Review** word with the same beginning sound.

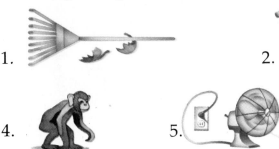

1.          2.          3.

4.          5.

**C** Write the **Challenge** word to complete each sentence.

1. Cooked meat and vegetables make a ____.
2. A hint is often called a ____.
3. Something worn on the foot is a ____.
4. A paper handkerchief is a ____.
5. Noon until evening is the ____.

## HANDWRITING HINTS

Be sure to form your letters carefully. If the final bump on an _m_ is not clear, the _m_ may look like an _n_ . Write *mule, broom,* and *moon.*

# Spelling and Writing: Adjectives

An *adjective* is a word that describes a noun. When you write sentences, you should always use the best adjective to tell about the noun. The adjective in each of these sentences is underlined.

The bird has <u>small</u> feathers.
The bird has <u>tiny</u> feathers.

The adjectives *small* and *tiny* mean almost the same thing, but *tiny* more closely tells about the noun.

## Writing Sentences

Think about the pet bird. Write a sentence that describes the bird. Write a sentence that describes the cage. Use a list word in each sentence, such as *new* or *few*.

## Editing sentencess

Replace each underlined adjective with an adjective that more closely describes the noun. Use the symbols to edit the sentences. Write your edited sentences.

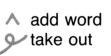

∧ add word
℺ take out

1. The bird sings a <s>nice</s> tune.　　2. I drew a <u>good</u> picture.

Now edit the sentences you wrote in **Writing Sentences.**

☐ Does each sentence have the best adjective? ☐ Are all the words spelled correctly?

# Review

What letters are missing? Complete each **New**, **Review**, and **Challenge** word. Write the word.

**A**
1. fl__
2. sp__n
3. gr__
4. n__
5. dr__
6. m_l_
7. t_n_
8. f__
9. br__m
10. r__t

**B**
1. p__l
2. f__d
3. z__
4. r__m
5. m__n

**C**
1. cl__
2. st__
3. sh__
4. tiss__
5. aftern__n

# Dictionary Skills

In a dictionary, each *entry word* is followed by the *pronunciation*, which shows how to say the word. Then the *meaning* and sometimes an *example sentence* are given.

pronunciation

meaning

**mule** (mūl)   An animal that is part horse and part donkey. *The mule pulled the plow for the farmer.*

entry word

example sentence

Find the word *broom* in your Spelling Dictionary. Then write the answers to these questions.

1. Which sound does *broom* have: /ū/ or /ü/?
2. How many meanings are shown for *broom*?
3. Is an example sentence shown for *broom*?

# Content Words

You may use these /ū/ words in your social studies class.

   **useful**    **statue**    **museum**

Write a word to complete each sentence. Use the Spelling Dictionary for help.

1. A building that shows many things is a ____.
2. Something that is helpful is ____.
3. A likeness of a person made of clay is a ____.

# THE /g/ and /j/ SOUNDS

/g/ is spelled **g** as in *goat*
/j/ is spelled **j** as in *jet*
   **g** as in *cage*

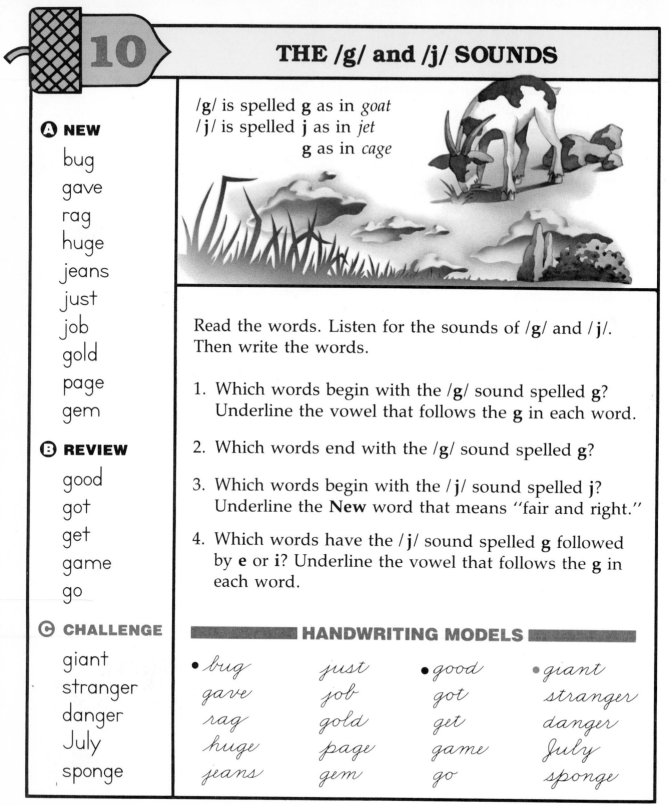

## A NEW

bug
gave
rag
huge
jeans
just
job
gold
page
gem

## B REVIEW

good
got
get
game
go

## C CHALLENGE

giant
stranger
danger
July
sponge

Read the words. Listen for the sounds of /**g**/ and /**j**/.
Then write the words.

1. Which words begin with the /**g**/ sound spelled **g**?
   Underline the vowel that follows the **g** in each word.

2. Which words end with the /**g**/ sound spelled **g**?

3. Which words begin with the /**j**/ sound spelled **j**?
   Underline the **New** word that means "fair and right."

4. Which words have the /**j**/ sound spelled **g** followed
   by **e** or **i**? Underline the vowel that follows the **g** in
   each word.

### HANDWRITING MODELS

| | | | |
|---|---|---|---|
| • bug | just | • good | • giant |
| gave | job | got | stranger |
| rag | gold | get | danger |
| huge | page | game | July |
| jeans | gem | go | sponge |

# Practice

**A** Write a **New** word to complete each sentence.

1. My ring is made of ___ .
2. Turn to the first ___ in the book.
3. A tiny ___ flew onto your arm.
4. Ann ___ me a present.
5. Mom wiped it with a ___ .
6. That is ___ the right size.
7. The whale is a ___ mammal.
8. The ruby is my favorite ___ .
9. Tomorrow I begin a new ___ .
10. Rita has a new pair of ___ .

**B** Read each sentence. Write a **Review** word that can be used in place of the underlined word.

1. Pam <u>climbed</u> up the hill.
2. Jean may <u>take</u> the prize.
3. Kathy was in the <u>contest</u>.
4. Jane has to <u>leave</u>.
5. The soup tastes <u>fine</u>.

**C** What letter is missing, **g** or **j**? Write a **Challenge** word to complete each sentence.

1. There's a spon_e in the sink.
2. She must be a stran_er here.
3. The story is about a _iant.
4. Today is the Fourth of _uly.
5. The lady yelled, "Dan_er!"

# Word History

Many words come from other languages. The word *gem* comes from the Latin *gemma*. Choose a word from the list. Look it up in a dictionary to find its history.

# Spelling and Writing: Similes

A *simile* tells how two different things are like one another by using *like* or *as*.

His yellow hair looks <u>like</u> gold.
His jeans are <u>as</u> blue <u>as</u> the sky.

# Writing Sentences

Imagine you are sailing on the sea. Write two similes that compare the sea with something else. Use *like* or *as* in each sentence. Use a list word in each sentence, such as *huge* or *gem*.

# Editin^g sentencess̶e̶

| |
|---|
| ∧ add words |

Write each sentence below as a simile. Use the words *like* or *as* in each sentence. Use the symbol to edit the sentences. Write your edited sentences.

1. The gem shines.    2. The bug moves slowly.

Now edit the sentences you wrote in **Writing Sentences.**

☐ Does each simile use the words *like* or *as?* ☐ Are all the words spelled correctly?

# Review

Write **g** or **j** to complete each **New, Review,** or **Challenge** word.

**Ⓐ** 1. bu_       6. _ave        **Ⓑ** 1. _ood       **Ⓒ** 1. _iant
    2. hu_e       7. _eans           2. _ot            2. stran_er
    3. ra_        8. _old            3. _et            3. dan_er
    4. _ust       9. _ob             4. _ame           4. _uly
    5. pa_e      10. _em             5. _o             5. spon_e

# Dictionary Skills

Each dictionary has a *pronunciation key.* The key shows how to say a word. For example, the pronunciation of the word *gave* is /**gāv**/. How do you pronounce the /ā/ sound? Look at the pronunciation key on the right. The /ā/ sound is pronounced like the sound in *cake*. The word *gave* has the same sound.

Read the first word in each row. Use the key to write each correct pronunciation.

| Key |  |
|---|---|
| a | b**a**d |
| ā | c**a**ke |
| ch | **ch**in |
| e | p**e**t |
| ē | m**e** |
| i | **i**t |
| ī | **i**ce |
| k | **k**it |
| o | n**o**t |
| ō | **o**pen |
| s | **s**it |
| sh | **sh**ip |
| th | **th**in |
| u | c**u**p |

1. **page**    /paj/      /pāj/      /poj/      pāj
2. **game**    /gām/      /gam/      /gim/
3. **job**     /jōb/      /jab/      /job/
4. **hole**    /hol/      /hōl/      /hil/
5. **mile**    /mil/      /mol/      /mīl/

# Content Words

You may use these /**g**/ and /**j**/ words in your science class.

   **gas   jet   geese**

Write the word that could join each group. Use the Spelling Dictionary for help.

1. ducks, swans, chickens, _____
2. plane, helicopter, balloon, _____
3. oil, water, coal, _____

# THE /s/ and /k/ SOUNDS

cute
send
truck
keep
since
book
price
us
dress
glass

can
see
soon
yes
seem

city
guess
circus
center
twice

/s/ is spelled **s** as in *sun*
**c** as in *cent*
**ss** as in *grass*
/k/ is spelled **k** as in *king*
**c** as in *cat*
**ck** as in *black*

Read the words. Listen for the sounds of /**s**/ and /**k**/.
Then write the words.

1. Which word has the /**k**/ sound spelled **ck** or **k**?

2. Which words have the /**k**/ sound spelled **c**?

3. Which words have the /**s**/ sound spelled **s**?
Underline the **New** words with the **s** spelling.

4. Which words have the /**s**/ sound spelled **ss**?

5. Which words have the /**s**/ sound spelled **c** followed
by **e** or **i**? Circle the **New** word with two /**s**/ sounds.

**▬▬▬▬ HANDWRITING MODELS ▬▬▬▬**

| | | | |
|---|---|---|---|
| •cute | book | •can | •city |
| send | price | see | guess |
| truck | us | soon | circus |
| keep | dress | yes | center |
| since | glass | seem | twice |

# Practice

**A** Write the **New** word that completes the sentence.

1. Pam wore a new ___ to the dance.
2. What is the ___ of that record?
3. Carl has been gone ___ yesterday.
4. Be sure to ___ the puppy warm.
5. There are fifty pages in the ___.
6. Pour the milk into a ___.
7. Please ___ it by mail.
8. I have a toy ___.
9. You look ___ in that suit.
10. Mike is not coming with ___.

**B** Name each picture. Write the **Review** word with the same ending sound.

1. 
2. 
3. 
4. 
5. 

**C** Read the clues. Write the **Challenge** word to match each clue. The word in the box gives the answer to this riddle.

**Riddle:** What do you call a matched pair?

1. a large town          _ _ | _ | _
2. two times             _ | _ _ _ _
3. group of performers   _ | _ _ _ _ _
4. the middle            _ _ | _ _ _
5. imagine               _ _ _ | _ | _

## Spelling Clues

How can you remember that <u>price</u> is spelled *price*, not *prise*? Think of this hint:

*What is the <u>price</u> of <u>rice</u>?*

Now choose another word from the list. Think of a way to remember its spelling.

*Practice* 43

# Spelling and Writing: A Descriptive Paragraph

PET SHOP

KITTEN FOR SALE

A *descriptive paragraph* tells what something or someone is like. This kind of paragraph can tell how something looks. It can tell how something tastes or feels. It may even tell how something smells or sounds.

Read this paragraph. The first sentence tells the main idea.

Jane picks a yellow flower. The petals feel very soft. They have a sweet smell. The flower waves in the wind.

## Writing a Paragraph

Think about the kitten in the pet shop. Write a descriptive paragraph that tells about the kitten. First write this main idea sentence: *We see an orange kitten.* Then write three detail sentences. Use at least three list words, such as *cute*, *keep*, or *glass*.

## Editing a paragraph

Use these symbols to edit your paragraph. Write your edited paragraph.

≡ make a capital letter
ℛ take out
∧ add words

☐ Does each detail sentence tell more about the main idea? ☐ Does each sentence start with a capital letter? ☐ Does each sentence end with a period?
☐ Are all the words spelled correctly?

# Review

What letters are missing? Write each word.

**Ⓐ**
1. gla_ _
2. sin_e
3. _ute
4. dre_ _
5. boo_
6. _end
7. u_
8. tru_ _
9. pri_e
10. _eep

**Ⓑ**
1. _oon
2. _an
3. _eem
4. _ee
5. ye_

**Ⓒ**
1. _ircus
2. _enter
3. _ity
4. gue_ _
5. twi_e

# Word Building

**If a word ends with _-s_, _-ss_, _-x_, _-sh_, or _-ch_, add _-es_ to name more than one.**

| gas | dress | box | dish | rich |
|-----|-------|-----|------|------|
| gases | dresses | boxes | dishes | riches |

Add the ending to each word. Write the complete word.

1. Tom has six (class + es) in school.  classes
2. Linda does two (wash + es) this morning.
3. Many (fox + es) run in the forest.
4. Jim sees three new (watch + es).

# Content Words

You may use these /s/ and /k/ words in your math class.

**distance     check     cube**

Write the word to complete each sentence. Use the Spelling Dictionary for help.

1. A solid figure with six equal sides is a ____ .
2. A mark put next to a right answer is a ____ .
3. The amount of space between things is a ____ .

# UNIT 12   REVIEW: UNITS 7-11

## UNIT 7

/ī/ is spelled **i-e, i, y,** or **igh**

| I | flight | mile | bright | dry |
|---|--------|------|--------|-----|
| blind | high | try | drive | find |

What letters are missing? Write the complete word.

1. dr_v_
2. h___
3. br___t
4. fl___t
5. m_l_
6. tr_
7. f_nd
8. dr_
9. bl_nd
10. Write the word that is always a capital letter.

## UNIT 8

/ō/ is spelled **o, o-e, oa,** or **ow**

| own | hole | most | toad | drove |
|-----|------|------|------|-------|
| blow | stove | float | grow | no |

Read the clues. Write the word for each clue. The words in the box give the answer to this riddle.

**Riddle:** What does a young kid become?

1. The opposite of *yes* is ____ .
2. To have is to ____ .
3. George didn't walk, he ____ .
4. The greatest number is the ____ .
5. To play a horn you must ____ .
6. An animal like a frog is a ____ .
7. As you get bigger you ____ .
8. An opening could be a ____ .
9. When you drift on water you ____ .
10. You can cook on a ____ .

1. _ _
2. _ _ _
3. _ _ _ _
4. _ _ _ _
5. _ _ _
6. _ _ _
7. _ _ _ _
8. _ _ _ _
9. _ _ _ _
10. _ _ _ _ _

/ū/ and /ü/ are spelled **u-e** or **ew**
/ü/ is spelled **oo**

| root | few | grew | mule | flew |
| tune | spoon | new | broom | drew |

Name each picture. Write the word that rhymes with each.

1.

2.

3.

Name each picture. Write the words that rhyme with each.

4.
5.

6. 8.
7. 9.
   10.

/**g**/ is spelled **g**
/**j**/ is spelled **j** or **g**

| bug | just | gave | huge | jeans |
| gold | page | gem | job | rag |

What letter is missing? Write the complete word.

1. _ust
2. hu_e

3. _old
4. pa_e

Circle the hidden words.
Then write each word.

```
j e a n s
o g a v e
b u g o n
r a g e m
```

/s/ is spelled **s, c,** or **ss**
/k/ is spelled **c, k,** or **ck**

| cute | send | truck | keep | since |
|------|------|-------|------|-------|
| book | price | us | dress | glass |

Read each word. Write the word that rhymes.

1. luck
2. class
3. bus
4. prince
5. deep

6. mice
7. boot
8. bend
9. less
10. look

# Word Building

Add the ending to each word. Write the whole word.

1. Kathy set two (glass + es) on the table.  glasses
2. My little plant is (grow + ing).
3. The three (toad + s) hopped.
4. Cindy (try + ed) to draw a clown.
5. We are (drive + ing) to Kentucky.
6. The leaf is (float + ing) on the pond.
7. The paint (dry + s) quickly.
8. The doll has three (dress + es).
9. The (keep + er) feeds the animals.
10. Jack was (tune + ing) the piano.

Complete each sentence. Mark the word that is
spelled correctly.

1. John and ____ are going.          eye  ⓐ    I       ●
2. The cat climbed up ____.          high ⓐ    hi      ⓑ
3. The dog dug a ____.               hole ⓐ    whole   ⓑ
4. He did not ____ his book.         fined ⓐ   find    ⓑ
5. She has ____ place to play.       now  ⓐ    no      ⓑ
6. The bird ____ away.               flew ⓐ    flu     ⓑ
7. Mary has a ____ dress.            new  ⓐ    knew    ⓑ
8. Mom dusts with an old ____.       rage ⓐ    rag     ⓑ
9. John has a ____ truck.            hug  ⓐ    huge    ⓑ
10. I ____ saw Maria leave.          gust ⓐ    just    ⓑ
11. She has one ____ to read.        peg  ⓐ    page    ⓑ
12. The baby looks ____ in the hat.  cute ⓐ    cut     ⓑ
13. What is the ____ of the game?    prize ⓐ   price   ⓑ
14. Juan passed the notes to ____.   us   ⓐ    use     ⓑ

Read each word. Mark the word that is **not** spelled
correctly.

15. own   ⓐ    16. mile  ⓐ    17. moast ⓐ    18. gro   ⓐ
    rute  ●        few   ⓑ        gave  ⓑ        truck ⓑ
    bug   ©        sind  ©        drive ©        blind ©

19. mule  ⓐ    20. bright ⓐ   21. geans ⓐ    22. dry   ⓐ
    keep  ⓑ        drove  ⓑ       blow  ⓑ        book  ⓑ
    tode  ©        flite  ©       tune  ©        sinse ©

23. flote ⓐ    24. job   ⓐ    25. grow  ⓐ    26. glass ⓐ
    spoon ⓑ        drew  ⓑ        trigh ⓑ        dress ⓑ
    stove ©        jold  ©        broom ©        jem   ©

# THE /st/, /sk/, /sm/, /sn/ SOUNDS

sky
smell
skate
skip
stop
snap
snow
smoke
scale
smile

**B REVIEW**

start
state
step
stick
star

**C CHALLENGE**

snowfall
scare
ski
stone
snake

/**st**/ is spelled **st** as in *store*
/**sk**/ is spelled **sc** as in *scarf*
        **sk** as in *skirt*
/**sm**/ is spelled **sm** as in *smock*
/**sn**/ is spelled **sn** as in *sneakers*

Read the words. Listen for the sound of /**st**/, /**sk**/, /**sm**/, and /**sn**/. Then write the words.

1. Which words have the /**sk**/ sound spelled **sc**?

2. Which words have the /**sk**/ sound spelled **sk**?

3. Which words have the /**st**/ sound spelled **st**?
   Underline the **New** word that means "the opposite of go."

4. Which words have the /**sm**/ sound spelled **sm**?

5. Which words have the /**sn**/ sound spelled **sn**?
   Underline the **New** word that means "flakes of ice."

**HANDWRITING MODELS**

• *sky*      *snap*      • *start*     • *snowfall*
*smell*    *snow*      *state*     *scare*
*skate*    *smoke*     *step*      *ski*
*skip*     *scale*     *stick*     *stone*
*stop*     *smile*     *star*      *snake*

# Practice

**Ⓐ** Write a **New** word to complete each sentence.

1. We like to ___ on the ice.
2. I know how to hop and ___ .
3. Pam always has a ___ on her face.
4. We weighed it on the ___ .
5. The ___ came from the fire.
6. The ___ is very clear today.
7. The bread and cheese ___ good.
8. When the light is red you ___ .
9. It will ___ if you step on it.
10. When it is cold rain becomes ___ .

**Ⓑ** What letters are missing? Write each **Review** word.

1. __ick    2. __ep    3. __art    4. __ar    5. __ate

**Ⓒ** Read the clues. Write the **Challenge** word for each.
The word in the box gives the answer to this riddle.

**Riddle:** What do you call a broken branch?

1. fall of snow
2. small rock
3. used to ride over snow or water
4. to frighten
5. legless animal with scales

___ | _ | _ _ _ _ _ _ _ _
_ _ | _ | _ _
_ _ | _ | _
_ _ _ | _ | _

## HANDWRITING HINTS

Be sure to form your letters carefully. If the final loop on the _k_ is not carefully made, the _k_ may look like an _h_. Write *sky*, *skip*, and *skate*.

# Spelling and Writing: Proper Nouns

A *proper noun* is a noun that names a special person, place, or thing. Begin each important word in a proper noun with a capital letter.

Jack Star
Alan Smith
Jenny Sneed

Jack Star

Alan Smith

Jenny Sneed

## Writing Sentences

Think about spending a winter weekend in the country with some friends. Look at the pictures. Write three sentences that tell what each person does. Use a proper noun in each sentence. Use at least one list word in each sentence, such as *sky*, *snow*, or *smell*.

## Editing sentences

Use the symbol to edit these sentences. Write your edited sentences.

| ≡ make a capital letter |
| --- |

1. Now sue skates on the pond.
2. Then roger skips along.
3. bob silver smiles at me.

Now edit the sentences you wrote in **Writing Sentences.**

☐ Does each proper noun begin with a capital letter?
☐ Are all the words spelled correctly?

# Review

Write the **New, Review,** or **Challenge** word that rhymes with each word below.

**A** 1. mile
2. fly
3. tale
4. oak
5. bell
6. late
7. tip
8. no
9. nap
10. hop

**B** 1. car
2. cart
3. pick
4. pep
5. ate

**C** 1. tea
2. lake
3. care
4. bone
5. so tall

# Word Building

**If a word ends with consonant-vowel-consonant, double the final consonant and add _-ing_ or _-ed_.**

stop + ing = stopping    stop + ed = stopped

Add the ending to each word. Write the whole word.

1. The girls are (skip + ing) rope.
2. Jan (step + ed) carefully on the stones.
3. Jody (snap + ed) her fingers.
4. Kathy was (hop + ing) down the street.

# Content Words

You may use these /**st**/, /**sk**/, and /**sm**/ words in your science class.

**skeleton    steam    smooth**

Write the word to replace the underlined words. Use the Spelling Dictionary for help.

1. The new highway is very <u>even and flat</u>.
2. The doctor studied the <u>framework of bones</u>.
3. The engine runs on <u>boiled water</u>.

**A NEW**

belt
bent
melt
went
gift
mix
told
left
paint
wild

**B REVIEW**

six
kind
mind
sand
box

**C CHALLENGE**

fault
tax
built
drift
front

/ft/ is spelled **ft** as in *lift*
/nt/ is spelled **nt** as in *tent*
/ld/ is spelled **ld** as in *gold*

/lt/ is spelled **lt** as in *quilt*
/ks/ is spelled **x** as in *fox*

Read the words. Listen for the sounds of /**ft**/, /**nt**/, /**ld**/, /**lt**/, and /**ks**/. Then write the words.

1. Which words have the /**ld**/ sound spelled **ld**?

2. Which words have the /**ks**/ sound spelled **x**?

3. Which words have the /**lt**/ sound spelled **lt**?

4. Which words have the /**nt**/ sound spelled **nt**?
   Underline the **New** word that means "gone away."

5. Which words have the /**ft**/ sound spelled **ft**?

6. Which **Review** words have the /**nd**/ sound spelled **nd**?

━━━━━ **HANDWRITING MODELS** ━━━━━

| • belt | mix | • six | • fault |
|--------|------|--------|---------|
| bent | told | kind | tax |
| melt | left | mind | built |
| went | paint | sand | drift |
| gift | wild | box | front |

# Practice

**Ⓐ** Write the **New** word to complete each sentence.

1. The tiger is a ___ animal.
2. Juan put the ___ on his pants.
3. Mary will ___ the picture.
4. The spoon was ___ out of shape.
5. Turn right instead of ___.
6. The candle will ___ in the heat.
7. Jill ___ me the truth.
8. Tim ___ downtown by bus.
9. Do not ___ the two colors.
10. Kim bought a ___ for her mom.

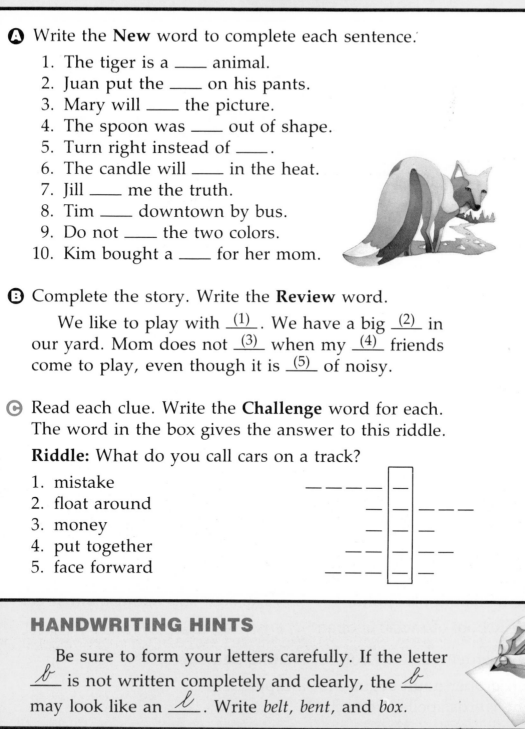

**Ⓑ** Complete the story. Write the **Review** word.

    We like to play with _(1)_ . We have a big _(2)_ in our yard. Mom does not _(3)_ when my _(4)_ friends come to play, even though it is _(5)_ of noisy.

**Ⓒ** Read each clue. Write the **Challenge** word for each. The word in the box gives the answer to this riddle.

**Riddle:** What do you call cars on a track?

1. mistake
2. float around
3. money
4. put together
5. face forward

— — — — —│—│
  —│—│— — —
  — — —│—│—
  — —│—│— —
  — — —│—│—

---

## HANDWRITING HINTS

    Be sure to form your letters carefully. If the letter _b_ is not written completely and clearly, the _b_ may look like an _l_ . Write *belt*, *bent*, and *box*.

# Spelling and Writing: Proper Nouns

A *proper noun* is a noun that names a special person, place, or thing. Begin each important word in a proper noun with a capital letter.

Center Zoo

Museum of Modern Art

Garden Library

Park School for Dance

## Writing Sentences

Imagine that friends visited your city. Look at the picture and signs. Write three sentences that tell about the different places they visit. Use a proper noun in each sentence. Use at least one list word in each sentence, such as *left, wild,* or *went.*

## Editin^g sentencess~e~

| ≡ make a capital letter |

Use the symbol to edit these sentences. Write your edited sentences.

1. Some ice melts in polar pond.

2. The davis school of music is open.

3. The sign tells about main street.

Now edit the sentences you wrote in **Writing Sentences.**

☐ Does each proper noun begin with a capital letter?
☐ Are all the words spelled correctly?

# Review

What letters are missing? Complete each **New, Review,** and **Challenge** word. Write each word.

**Ⓐ**
1. gi＿＿
2. be＿＿
3. me＿＿
4. we＿＿
5. to＿＿
6. wi＿＿
7. be＿＿
8. pai＿＿
9. mi＿
10. le＿＿

**Ⓑ**
1. bo＿
2. si＿
3. sa＿＿
4. ki＿＿
5. mi＿＿

**Ⓒ**
1. fro＿＿
2. ta＿
3. dri＿＿
4. fau＿＿
5. bui＿＿

# Dictionary Skills

Sometimes when you look up a word in the dictionary, it will have more than one meaning. Read the part of the dictionary. Notice that each word has more than one meaning.

Read each sentence. Write the correct meaning for the underlined word.

1. Henry used purple <u>paint</u>.
2. I will <u>paint</u> it pink.
3. Ann sang in the class <u>play</u>.

> **paint** /pānt/ *n.* matter with color used with a brush. *v.* to put on colored matter with a brush.
> **play** /plā/ *n.* **1.** a move in a game. **2.** a story acted on a stage. *v.* to do something to have fun.

# Content Words

You may use these /lt/, /nt/, and /ft/ words in your science class.

**colt     silent     lift**

Write a word to complete each sentence. Use the Spelling Dictionary for help.

1. The new machine can ＿＿ the hay.
2. The young ＿＿ eats the oats.
3. Barn animals are usually ＿＿ at night.

# 15

# THE /ô/ SOUND

/ô/ is spelled **a** as in *chalk*
**aw** as in *straw*

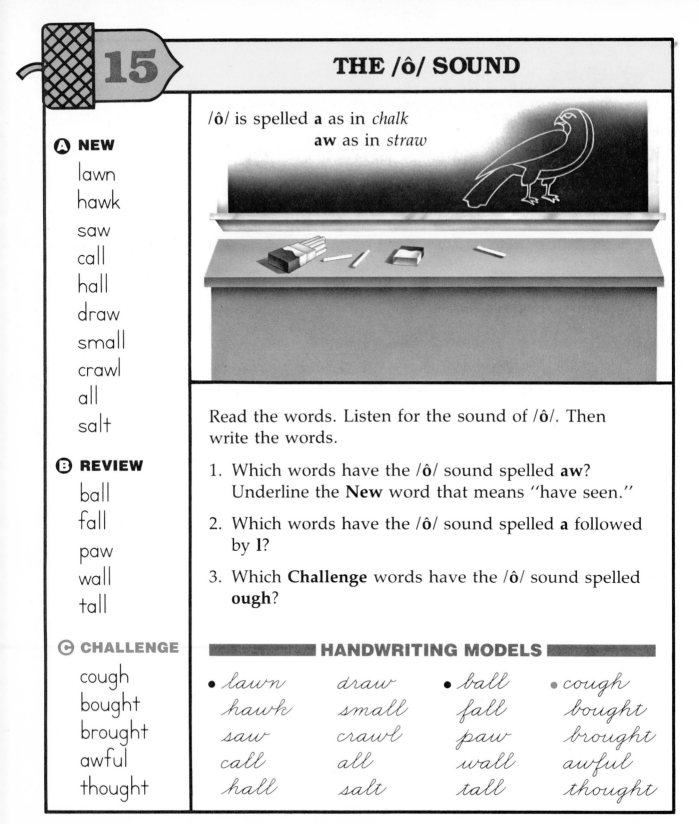

## Ⓐ NEW

lawn
hawk
saw
call
hall
draw
small
crawl
all
salt

## Ⓑ REVIEW

ball
fall
paw
wall
tall

## Ⓒ CHALLENGE

cough
bought
brought
awful
thought

Read the words. Listen for the sound of /ô/. Then write the words.

1. Which words have the /ô/ sound spelled **aw**? Underline the **New** word that means "have seen."

2. Which words have the /ô/ sound spelled **a** followed by **l**?

3. Which **Challenge** words have the /ô/ sound spelled **ough**?

### ▬ HANDWRITING MODELS ▬

- *lawn*   *draw*
  *hawk*   *small*
  *saw*   *crawl*
  *call*   *all*
  *hall*   *salt*

- *ball*
  *fall*
  *paw*
  *wall*
  *tall*

- *cough*
  *bought*
  *brought*
  *awful*
  *thought*

# Practice

**Ⓐ** Write a **New** word to complete each sentence.

1. Tomorrow I will mow the ＿＿.
2. Rita likes to ＿＿ with crayons.
3. We had to ＿＿ on our knees.
4. Mom will ＿＿ us on the phone.
5. There is too much ＿＿ in the soup.
6. Her room is down the ＿＿.
7. Dana is too ＿＿ to ride the bike.
8. We ＿＿ Maria at the store today.
9. Jean ate ＿＿ her dinner.
10. Look at the ＿＿ above the trees.

**Ⓑ** Write the correct **Review** words to complete the sentence.

The cat sat upon the very t_(1)_ w_(2)_ and watched the b_(3)_ f_(4)_ that it had knocked off with its p_(5)_.

**Ⓒ** Write the correct **Challenge** words to complete the sentence.

Mike t_(1)_ Ann br_(2)_ the medicine she'd b_(3)_ for his a_(4)_ c_(5)_.

## HANDWRITING HINTS

Be sure to form your letters carefully. If the ending stroke on a _w_ is not clear, the _w_ may look like a _u_. Write *lawn*, *hawk*, and *draw*.

# Spelling and Writing: A Telephone Message

If you answer a telephone call that is for someone else, you need to take a *message*. Read the message.

The message tells all the important information. The call was for *Kim Lee*. It was from *Bob Evans*. He called at *3:30 P.M.* He said that *The club will meet on Friday*. His number is *666-5867*. The message was taken by *Jane Fields*.

A call for: Kim Lee
Caller's name: Bob Evans
Time: 3:30 P.M.
Message: The club will meet on Friday.
Caller's number: 666-5867
Message taken by: Jane Fields

# Writing a Telephone Message

Imagine that you are taking a message for a friend named Dawn Small. Her friend Waldo Hall calls and wants Dawn to call him back at 774-3390. He says he needs Dawn to draw a picture of a small hawk on a lawn. You notice that the time is 4:15 P.M.

Use the information above to fill in the form.

A call for: ____
Caller's name: ____
Time: ____
Message: ____
Caller's number: ____
Message taken by: ____

Now edit the telephone message you wrote in the form.

☐ Is the information in the message correct? ☐ Are all the words spelled correctly?

# Review

What letters are missing? Write the words.

**Ⓐ**
1. dr__
2. sa__
3. l__n
4. s__
5. c__l
6. cr__l
7. __l
8. h__k
9. h__l
10. sm__l

**Ⓑ**
1. p__
2. f__l
3. b__l
4. w__l
5. t__l

**Ⓒ**
1. th____t
2. br____t
3. b____t
4. __ful
5. c____

# Word Building

**Add _-s_ to a word to tell what one person does.**

    walk + s = walks
    The boy <u>walks</u>.

Add the **-s** ending to each word. Write the complete word.

1. A girl (draw + s) a picture.
2. The man (look + s) at the picture.
3. The woman (give + s) her a prize.
4. The boy (clap + s) his hands.
5. The girl (smile + s) at them.

# Content Words

You may use these /ô/ words in your science class.

**claw    false    rainfall**

Write the word to complete each sentence. Use the Spelling Dictionary for help.

1. Water falling from the sky is ____.
2. A nail on the foot of a bird is a ____.
3. The opposite of true is ____.

# 16

# THE /ou/ and /oi/ SOUNDS

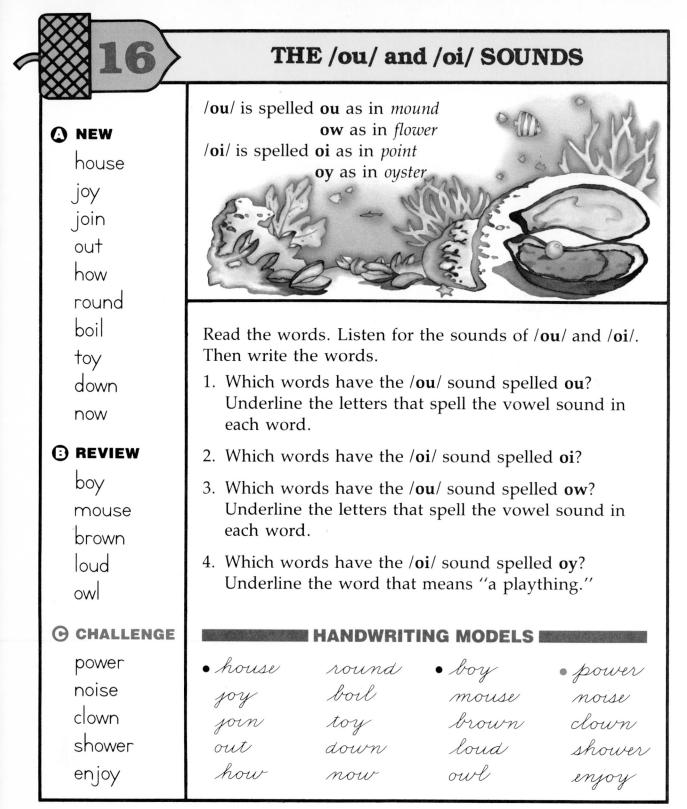

/**ou**/ is spelled **ou** as in *mound*
  **ow** as in *flower*
/**oi**/ is spelled **oi** as in *point*
  **oy** as in *oyster*

**A NEW**
house
joy
join
out
how
round
boil
toy
down
now

**B REVIEW**
boy
mouse
brown
loud
owl

**C CHALLENGE**
power
noise
clown
shower
enjoy

Read the words. Listen for the sounds of /**ou**/ and /**oi**/.
Then write the words.

1. Which words have the /**ou**/ sound spelled **ou**?
   Underline the letters that spell the vowel sound in
   each word.

2. Which words have the /**oi**/ sound spelled **oi**?

3. Which words have the /**ou**/ sound spelled **ow**?
   Underline the letters that spell the vowel sound in
   each word.

4. Which words have the /**oi**/ sound spelled **oy**?
   Underline the word that means "a plaything."

**━━ HANDWRITING MODELS ━━**

- *house*  *round*  • *boy*  • *power*
  *joy*  *boil*  *mouse*  *noise*
  *join*  *toy*  *brown*  *clown*
  *out*  *down*  *loud*  *shower*
  *how*  *now*  *owl*  *enjoy*

# Practice

**Ⓐ** Write the **New** word that rhymes with the underlined word to complete each sentence.

1. The toy he <u>found</u> was ____.
2. The <u>town</u> is ____ the road.
3. The <u>oil</u> began to ____.
4. At the <u>bout</u> he was knocked ____.
5. Jack paid a <u>coin</u> in order to ____.
6. <u>Now</u> Raúl must learn ____ to do it.
7. Little <u>Roy</u> likes his new ____.
8. A <u>mouse</u> ran around the ____.
9. The little <u>boy</u> jumped for ____.
10. What did the <u>cow</u> do ____?

**Ⓑ** What letters are missing? Write the **Review** word.

1. __l   2. br__n   3. b__   4. m__se   5. l__d

**Ⓒ** Read each clue. Write the **Challenge** word for each. The word in the box gives the answer to this riddle.

**Riddle:** What do a king and a rooster both have?

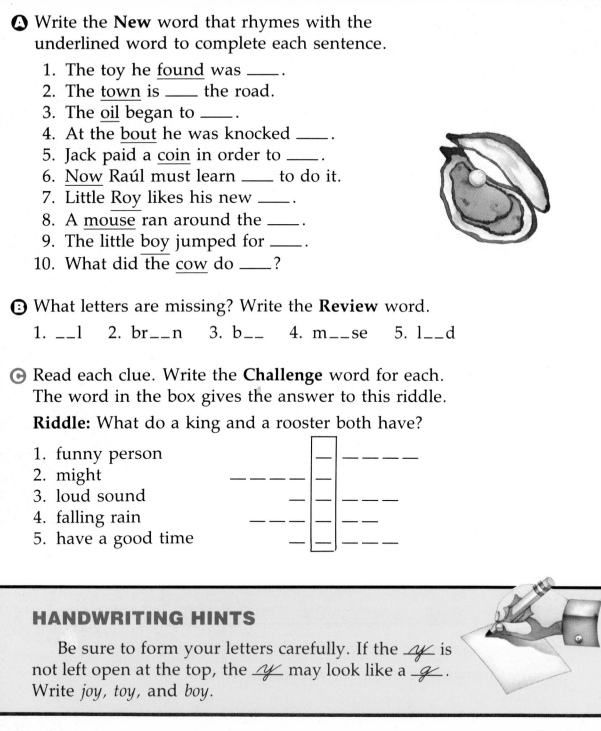

1. funny person      __ | __ __ __ __ __
2. might      __ __ __ __ | __
3. loud sound      __ | __ __ __ __
4. falling rain      __ __ __ | __ __
5. have a good time      __ | __ __ __

## HANDWRITING HINTS

Be sure to form your letters carefully. If the *y* is not left open at the top, the *y* may look like a *g*. Write *joy, toy,* and *boy.*

# Spelling and Writing: An Invitation

An *invitation* is a note sent to people you want to invite to a party. An invitation tells people what they need to know about the party. Read the invitation.

The invitation tells all the important information. The party is for *Carlos Ruiz.* It will be given at *10 Harbor Lane,* on *Saturday, June 20.* The time for the party is *1:00 P.M.* The telephone number, *444-9000,* is given so that people can call Carlos to ask about the party and tell him if they will be coming or not.

Please come to my birthday party.

**Name:** Carlos Ruiz

**Place:** 10 Harbor Lane

**Date:** Saturday

**Time:** 1:00 P.M.

**Telephone:** 444-9000

## Writing An Invitation

Imagine that you are having a party for your new house. Start your invitation with this sentence:

*Please join me for a party in my new house.*

Be sure to include all the important information.

**Name:** ____
**Place:** ____
**Date:** ____
**Time:** ____
**Telephone:** ____

Now edit the information you wrote.

☐ Is all the information correct?  ☐ Are all the words spelled correctly?

# Review

Write the **New, Review,** and **Challenge** words that complete the chart.

| /**ou**/ spelled: | | | | |
|---|---|---|---|---|
| **ou** | Ⓐ | | Ⓑ | |
| **ow** | Ⓐ | | Ⓑ | Ⓒ |
| | | | | |

| /**oi**/ spelled: | | | |
|---|---|---|---|
| **oi** | Ⓐ | | Ⓒ |
| **oy** | Ⓐ | Ⓑ | |

# Word Building

Sometimes knowing how to spell one word can help you spell other words. This is because many words may have the same *spelling pattern*. For example, the letters *-ound* are a spelling pattern. If you know how to spell *round*, you may figure out how to spell *sound*.

Add *-ound* to make new words. Write the words.

**-ound**  1. m _____  3. f _____  5. s _____
            2. p _____  4. gr _____  6. h _____

# Content Words

You may use these /**ou**/ and /**oi**/ words in your math class.

**amount**    **point**    **count**

Write a word to complete each sentence. Use the Spelling Dictionary for help.

1. A dot on a number line is a _____.
2. To say or write numbers in order is to _____.
3. The number something adds up to is an _____.

**A NEW**

today
before
ready
until
every
Sunday
Friday
morning
Halloween
Thanksgiving

**B REVIEW**

late
rain
mail
night
nice

**C CHALLENGE**

Thursday
during
Monday
second
evening

Some words tell about time and having happy days. It is important to know how to spell them.

Read and think about each word. Then write the word that matches each clue.

**A** 1. October 31
2. day to give thanks
3. this very day
4. day before Saturday
5. at an earlier time
6. early in the day
7. up to the time of
8. each
9. prepared
10. day after Saturday

**B** 1. very good
2. dark part of the day
3. letters and cards
4. not on time
5. drops of water
2. late in the day
4. fourth school day

**C** 1. first school day
3. in the time of
5. after first

### ▰▰ HANDWRITING MODELS ▰▰

- *today  Sunday*
  *before  Friday*
  *ready  morning*
  *until  Halloween*
  *every  Thanksgiving*

- *late  • Thursday*
  *rain  during*
  *mail  Monday*
  *night  second*
  *nice  evening*

# Practice

**A** Write a **New** word to complete each sentence.

1. Jack will be a clown for ____ .
2. We have a family dinner every ____ .
3. The day after Saturday is ____ .
4. The day before Saturday is ____ .
5. The bus won't arrive ____ noon.
6. The day ____ Sunday is Saturday.
7. Jane is always ____ to go.
8. John leaves at 8:00 A. M. ____ day.
9. I will go to the store later ____ .
10. We get up at 6:30 A. M. in the ____ .

**B** Complete each sentence with a **Review** word.

1. I hope it does not ____ .
2. Jack will be a little ____ .
3. Jan is a very ____ person.
4. Mary will ____ the letter.
5. We go to bed at 8:00 each ____ .

**C** Read the clues. Write the **Challenge** word for each.

1. Saturday, Sunday, ____
2. first, ____ , third
3. morning, afternoon, ____
4. while, at the same time as, ____
5. Tuesday, Wednesday, ____

# Word History

Many words come from other languages. The word *Monday* comes from the Latin *lunae dies* and means "moon's day."

Choose a day of the week from the list. Look in a dictionary to find its history.

# **Spelling and Writing:** Directions

*Directions* tell you how to do things. Directions can tell you how to get somewhere. Good directions make sense. You should give each step of the directions in the right order.

Read the following directions.

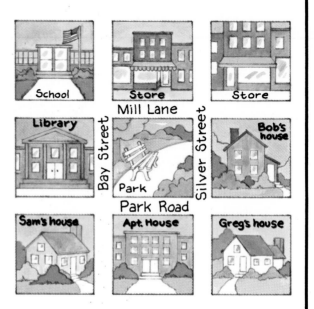

> You can get from Bob's house to the school.
> First walk up Silver Avenue to Mill Lane.
> Next turn left at Mill Lane.
> Last walk to the school.

# Writing Directions

Imagine someone asks you how to get from Greg's house to the library. Use the map above. Use words like *first*, *next*, and *last* to begin each sentence. Begin the directions with the following sentence.

*You can go from Greg's house to the library.*

Now edit the directions you wrote.

☐ Do the directions make sense? ☐ Are the directions in the right order? ☐ Are all the words spelled correctly? ☐ Do all the proper nouns begin with capital letters?

# Review

What letters are missing? Complete each **New, Review,** and **Challenge** word. Write the word.

**Ⓐ** 1. Th_nksg_ving
2. t_d__
3. r__dy
4. _v_ry
5. Fr_d__
6. S_nd__
7. b_f_r_

8. H_llow__n
9. m_rn_ng
10. _nt_l

**Ⓑ** 1. n_c_
2. l_t_
3. m__l
4. n___t

5. r__n

**Ⓒ** 1. Th_rsd__
2. _v_n_ng
3. M_nd__
4. d_r_ng
5. s_c_nd

# Dictionary Skills

Words in a dictionary are in ABC order. When a set of words begins with the same letter, use the second letter to put the words in ABC order.

Write these words in ABC order.

1. night   now   name
2. room   ready   rain
3. low   left   late

ate, are, ask
are
ask
ate

# Content Words

You may use these words in your reading class.

**adventure   calendar   after**

Write the word that could be in each group. Use the Spelling Dictionary for help.

1. date, year, month, ____
2. trip, travel, vacation, ____
3. in the rear, back, behind, ____

# UNIT 18   REVIEW: UNITS 13-17

## UNIT 13

/st/ is spelled **st**; /sk/ is spelled **sc** or **sk**
/sm/ is spelled **sm**; /sn/ is spelled **sn**

| | | | | |
|---|---|---|---|---|
| smoke | smell | skate | skip | stop |
| snow | snap | sky | scale | smile |

Name each picture. Write the words that have the same
beginning sound.

## UNIT 14

/ft/ is spelled **ft**; /nt/ is spelled **nt**; /ld/ is spelled **ld**
/lt/ is spelled **lt**; /ks/ is spelled **x**

| | | | | |
|---|---|---|---|---|
| belt | bent | melt | went | gift |
| mix | told | left | paint | wild |

What letter is missing from each pair of words? Write
each word.

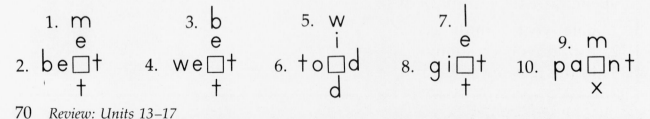

/ô/ is spelled **a** or **aw**

| | | | | |
|---|---|---|---|---|
| lawn | hawk | saw | call | hall |
| draw | small | crawl | all | salt |

**A.** Read the words in the box.

> hall   saw   call   small   crawl

Write them in ABC order.

**B.** Read each clue. Write the word for each clue.

1. grass
2. bird
3. to color
4. every
5. pepper and ____

/**ou**/ is spelled **ou** or **ow**
/**oi**/ is spelled **oi** or **oy**

| | | | | |
|---|---|---|---|---|
| house | joy | join | out | how |
| round | boil | toy | down | now |

Find the hidden words in the puzzle.
Then write the word.

| | | | | |
|---|---|---|---|---|
| a | j | o | i | n |
| h | o | u | s | e |
| o | y | t | b | r |
| w | n | d | o | o |
| t | o | o | i | u |
| o | w | w | l | n |
| y | x | n | z | d |

Some words we use tell about time and having happy days.

| today | Halloween | ready | morning | every |
|-------|-----------|-------|---------|-------|
| Sunday | Friday | until | before | Thanksgiving |

What letters are missing? Complete the puzzle. The word in the box gives the answer to this riddle.

**Riddle:** What is a hungry elephant's favorite time of the day?

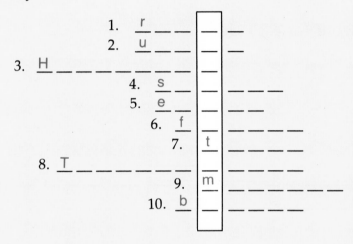

1. r _ _ _ | _ | _
2. u _ _ | _ | _
3. H _ _ _ _ _ _ _ | _ |
4. s _ | _ | _ _ _
5. e _ | _ | _ _ _
6. f _ | _ | _ _ _ _
7. | t | _ _ _ _
8. T _ _ _ _ _ _ | _ | _ _ _ _
9. | m | _ _ _ _ _ _
10. b _ | _ | _ _ _ _

# Word Building

**If a word ends with consonant-vowel-consonant, double the final consonant and add *-ing* or *-ed*.**

skip + ing = skipping    skip + ed = skipped

Add the ending to each word. Write the complete word.

1. The girls were (run + ing) to the lake.
2. They liked (get + ing) wet.
3. The boys were (swim + ing), too.
4. Susan (rub + ed) her eyes.
5. Robert (tap + ed) the ball.

Look at the words in each group. One word is misspelled. Mark the word that is not spelled correctly.

1. ⓐ smoke
   ⓑ now
   ⊙ evry

2. ⓐ whent
   ⓑ snow
   ⓒ hawk

3. ⓐ sky
   ⓑ lawn
   ⓒ skale

4. ⓐ saw
   ⓑ befor
   ⓒ call

5. ⓐ rede
   ⓑ stop
   ⓒ belt

6. ⓐ wild
   ⓑ doun
   ⓒ bent

7. ⓐ melt
   ⓑ bant
   ⓒ how

8. ⓐ hall
   ⓑ balt
   ⓒ out

9. ⓐ snap
   ⓑ col
   ⓒ hawk

10. ⓐ Sunday
    ⓑ Firday
    ⓒ left

11. ⓐ boil
    ⓑ miks
    ⓒ skip

12. ⓐ skate
    ⓑ melt
    ⓒ lown

13. ⓐ houes
    ⓑ saw
    ⓒ join

14. ⓐ moring
    ⓑ snap
    ⓒ scale

15. ⓐ sky
    ⓑ untill
    ⓒ every

16. ⓐ gift
    ⓑ hou
    ⓒ draw

17. ⓐ round
    ⓑ smell
    ⓒ aut

18. ⓐ smal
    ⓑ paint
    ⓒ toy

19. ⓐ nou
    ⓑ told
    ⓒ joy

20. ⓐ smok
    ⓑ mix
    ⓒ Halloween

21. ⓐ today
    ⓑ drow
    ⓒ went

22. ⓐ crawl
    ⓑ salt
    ⓒ smil

23. ⓐ all
    ⓑ house
    ⓒ crall

24. ⓐ holl
    ⓑ smile
    ⓒ Thanksgiving

# 19 THE /n/, /r/, /f/, /m/ SOUNDS

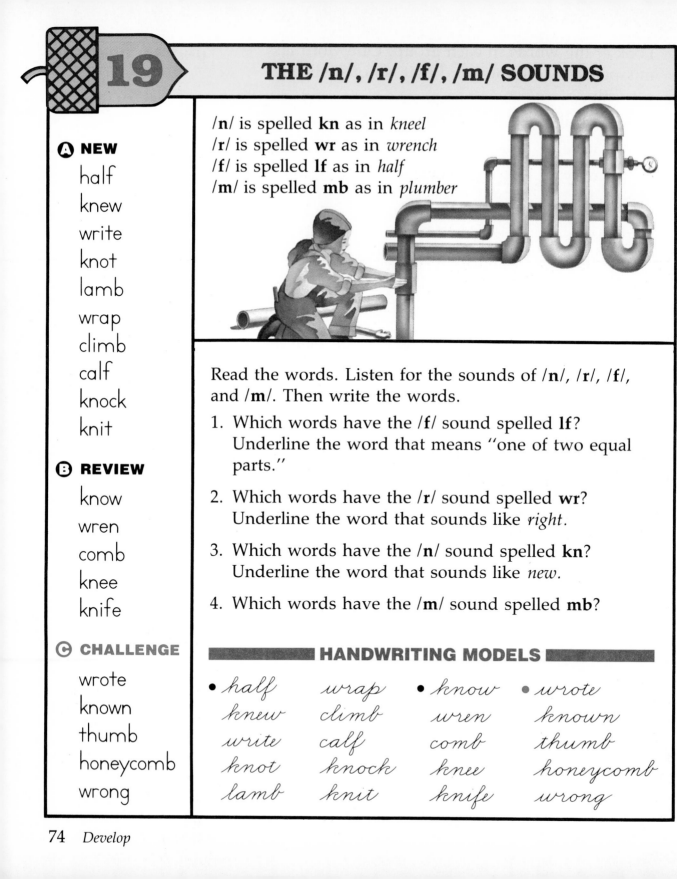

**Ⓐ NEW**

half
knew
write
knot
lamb
wrap
climb
calf
knock
knit

**Ⓑ REVIEW**

know
wren
comb
knee
knife

**Ⓒ CHALLENGE**

wrote
known
thumb
honeycomb
wrong

/n/ is spelled **kn** as in *kneel*
/r/ is spelled **wr** as in *wrench*
/f/ is spelled **lf** as in *half*
/m/ is spelled **mb** as in *plumber*

Read the words. Listen for the sounds of /n/, /r/, /f/, and /m/. Then write the words.

1. Which words have the /f/ sound spelled **lf**? Underline the word that means "one of two equal parts."

2. Which words have the /r/ sound spelled **wr**? Underline the word that sounds like *right*.

3. Which words have the /n/ sound spelled **kn**? Underline the word that sounds like *new*.

4. Which words have the /m/ sound spelled **mb**?

**HANDWRITING MODELS**

• *half*    *wrap*    • *know*    • *wrote*
*knew*    *climb*    *wren*    *known*
*write*    *calf*    *comb*    *thumb*
*knot*    *knock*    *knee*    *honeycomb*
*lamb*    *knit*    *knife*    *wrong*

# Practice

**A** What letters are missing? Write the **New** word.

1. I heard a __ock at the door.
2. The cow had a new ca__.
3. We saw a la__ at the farm.
4. John __ew the answer.
5. I must __ite to my sister.

6. Mother __it a scarf for me.
7. Ed had a __ot in his shoelace.
8. We will cli__ to the top.
9. Ann drank ha__ a glass of milk.
10. I will __ap the gift for Mary.

**B** Write the **Review** word to complete each sentence.

1. Cut the meat with your ___!
2. I don't ___ the story.
3. A ___ is a small, brown bird.
4. Fix your hair with the ___.
5. He put a patch on his ___.

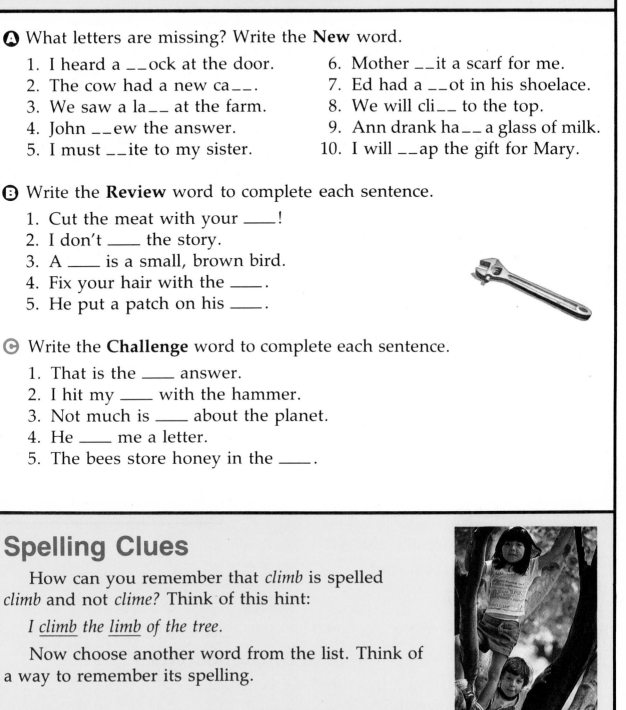

**C** Write the **Challenge** word to complete each sentence.

1. That is the ___ answer.
2. I hit my ___ with the hammer.
3. Not much is ___ about the planet.
4. He ___ me a letter.
5. The bees store honey in the ___.

## Spelling Clues

How can you remember that *climb* is spelled *climb* and not *clime?* Think of this hint:

*I climb the limb of the tree.*

Now choose another word from the list. Think of a way to remember its spelling.

A *possessive noun* names who or what has something. Add an *apostrophe* and *s* (**'s**) to a word that does not end with *s*.

land of the <u>farmer</u> = <u>farmer's</u> land

Add an *apostrophe* to a word that ends with *s*.

land of the <u>farmers</u> = <u>farmers'</u> land

# Writing Sentences

Choose the correct possessive noun. Then write the complete sentence.

1. Two ____ meals are ready.     a. lamb's     b. lambs'
2. We clean a ____ dish.     a. calf's     b. calfs'

# Editing sentences

Use the symbols to edit these sentences. Write your edited sentences.

1. I knock on two farmers doors.

2. I know two horses names.

3. we wrap the horses leg.

4. I climb a farmers tree.

| | |
|---|---|
| ∨ | apostrophe |
| ≡ | make a capital letter |

Now edit the sentences you wrote in **Writing Sentences**.

☐ Are the possessive nouns written correctly? ☐ Are all words spelled correctly?

# Review

Write the **New**, **Review**, and **Challenge** words that complete the chart.

| /n/ spelled **kn** | | /r/ spelled **wr** | /m/ spelled **mb** |
|---|---|---|---|
| Ⓐ | | Ⓐ | Ⓐ |
| | | | |
| | Ⓒ | Ⓑ | Ⓑ |
| | | Ⓒ | Ⓒ |
| Ⓓ | | | |

Write the words that rhyme with *laugh*.　　1. ____　　　2. ____

# Word Building

　　A *prefix* is a letter or group of letters added to the beginning of a word to make a new word. Read the following prefixes and their meanings:

| Prefix | Meaning | Example |
|---|---|---|
| un-<br>re- | do the opposite of<br>again | unwrap (do the opposite of wrap)<br>rewrite (write again) |

Write each word that replaces the underlined words.

1. I <u>do the opposite of knot</u> the string.　　unknot
2. The girls <u>climb again</u> the tree.
3. Jody will <u>wrap again</u> the gift.
4. The boys <u>do the opposite of snap</u> their jackets.

# Content Words

You may use these /r/ words in your English class.

　　**wrinkle**　　**written**　　**writing**

Write the word to complete each sentence.

1. He is ____ a story about his dog.
2. The book was ____ many years ago.
3. His shirt did not have a ____ .

# 20 THE /ch/, /th/, /sh/, /hw/ SOUNDS

## A NEW

while
path
which
three
they
much
child
wish
with
ship

## B REVIEW

them
then
when
white
than

## C CHALLENGE

cherry
thirty
shadow
everything
thirsty

/ch/ is spelled **ch** as in *children*
/th/ is spelled **th** as in *cloth*
/sh/ is spelled **sh** as in *wash*
/hw/ is spelled **wh** as in *wheel*

Read the words. Listen for the sounds of /**ch**/, /**th**/, /**sh**/, and /**hw**/. Then write the words.

1. Which words have the /**hw**/ sound spelled **wh**? Underline the **New** word that means "what one."

2. Which words have the /**th**/ sound spelled **th**? Underline the **th** in each **New** word.

3. Which words have the /**ch**/ sound spelled **ch**? Underline the **ch** in each **New** word.

4. Which words have the /**sh**/ sound spelled **sh**?

### ■ HANDWRITING MODELS ■

| • while | much | • them | • cherry |
|---------|-------|--------|----------|
| path | child | then | thirty |
| which | wish | when | shadow |
| three | with | white | everything |
| they | ship | than | thirsty |

# Practice

**A** Write the missing **New** word to complete the story.

    One day a young c_(1)_ walked w_(2)_ her dog down a p_(3)_, w_(4)_ led to the beach. In the distance she could see t_(5)_ kinds of boats: a sailboat, a huge s_(6)_, and a fishing boat. She said, w_(7)_ t_(8)_ walked along, "I w_(9)_ we had a boat of our own. It I would be so m_(10)_ fun!"

**B** Write the **Review** word to complete each sentence.

1. I like this one more ____ that.
2. Please tell me ____ it comes.
3. We'll eat first and ____ go.
4. I saw ____ just the other day.
5. I have a red and ____ tie.

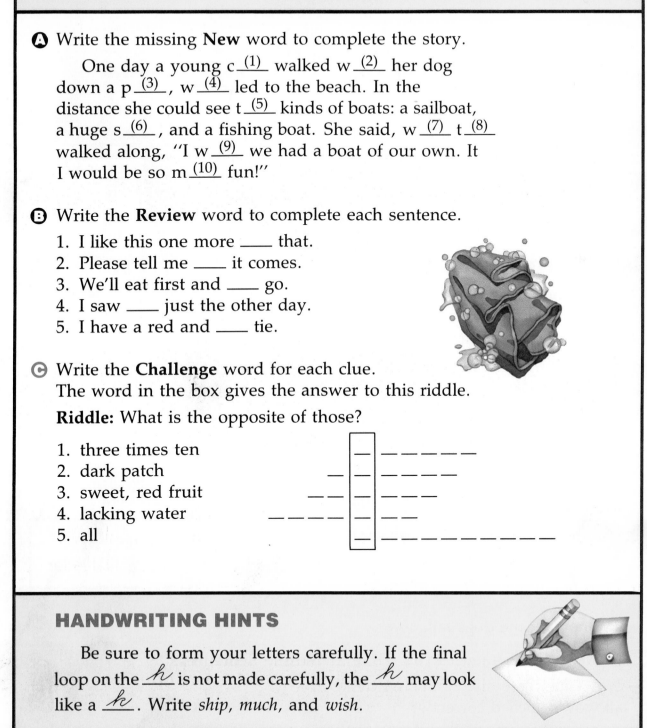

**C** Write the **Challenge** word for each clue.
The word in the box gives the answer to this riddle.

**Riddle:** What is the opposite of those?

1. three times ten
2. dark patch
3. sweet, red fruit
4. lacking water
5. all

## HANDWRITING HINTS

    Be sure to form your letters carefully. If the final loop on the _h_ is not made carefully, the _h_ may look like a _k_. Write *ship*, *much*, and *wish*.

# Spelling and Writing: Possessive Nouns

A *possessive noun* names who or what has something. Add an *apostrophe* and *s* ('s) to a word that does not end with *s*.

mask of the <u>girl</u> = <u>girl's</u> mask

Add an *apostrophe* to a word that ends with *s*.

masks of the <u>girls</u> = <u>girls'</u> masks

# Writing Sentences

Think about a Halloween party. Write three sentences that tell about the party. Use each possessive noun below in one of your sentences. Also, in each sentence, use one list word, such as *three, they,* or *with*.

1. boys' masks
2. pumpkin's face
3. girl's game

# Editing sentences

Use the symbols to edit these sentences. Write your edited sentences.

1. three girls hats were white.

2. They pat the dogs tail.

| | |
|---|---|
| ⌄ | apostrophe |
| ≡ | make a capital letter |

Now edit the sentences you wrote in **Writing Sentences**.

☐ Are all possessive nouns written correctly? ☐ Are all words spelled correctly?

# Review

What letters are missing? Complete each **New**, **Review**, and **Challenge** word. Write the word.

**Ⓐ**
1. __ip
2. __ile
3. wi__
4. pa__
5. __ich

6. __ild
7. __ree
8. mu__
9. __ey
10. wi__

**Ⓑ**
1. __en
2. __em
3. __an
4. __ite
5. __en

**Ⓒ**
1. __irty
2. __adow
3. __erry
4. __irsty
5. every__ing

# Word Building

**If a word ends with _s, ss, x, sh,_ or _ch,_ add _-es_ to tell what one person does.**

> wish + es = wishes
> The child <u>wishes</u> for good weather.

Add the ending to each word. Write the complete word.

1. Gail (dress + es) for school.   dresses
2. Jim (cross + es) the street.
3. A man (watch + es) the cars.
4. The girl (rush + es) in the rain.
5. A woman (guess + es) the time.
6. Cindy (catch + es) a cold.

# Content Words

You may use these /**ch**/ and /**sh**/ words in your math class.

**chart      shape      inch**

Write the word to complete each sentence. Use the Spelling Dictionary for help.

1. The line was only an ____ long.
2. Both circles are the same size and ____.
3. He kept a ____ of the money he earned.

# THE /ng/ and /kw/ SOUNDS

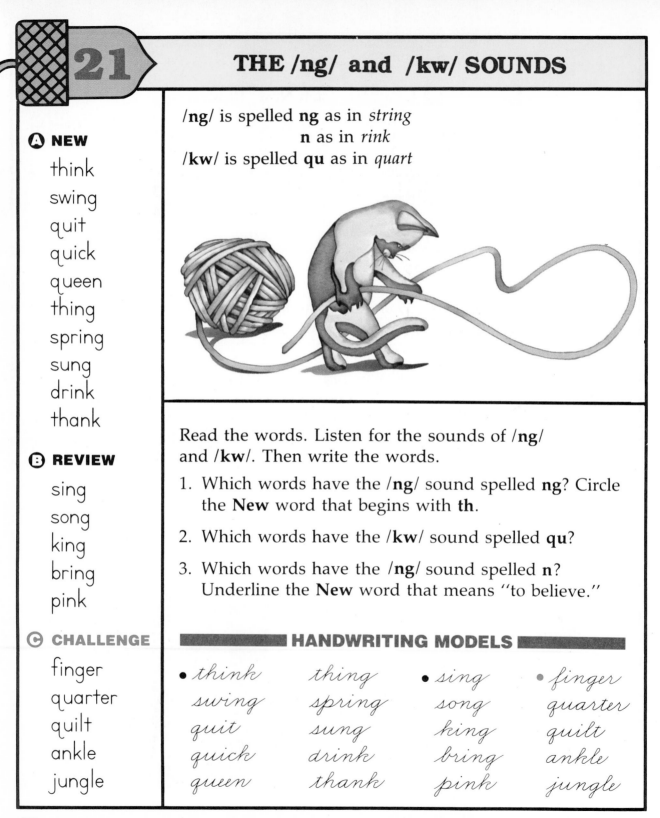

/**ng**/ is spelled **ng** as in *string*
**n** as in *rink*
/**kw**/ is spelled **qu** as in *quart*

## Ⓐ NEW

think
swing
quit
quick
queen
thing
spring
sung
drink
thank

## Ⓑ REVIEW

sing
song
king
bring
pink

## Ⓒ CHALLENGE

finger
quarter
quilt
ankle
jungle

Read the words. Listen for the sounds of /**ng**/ and /**kw**/. Then write the words.

1. Which words have the /**ng**/ sound spelled **ng**? Circle the **New** word that begins with **th**.

2. Which words have the /**kw**/ sound spelled **qu**?

3. Which words have the /**ng**/ sound spelled **n**? Underline the **New** word that means "to believe."

### ▰ HANDWRITING MODELS ▰

- *think*　　*thing*　　• *sing*　　• *finger*
*swing*　　*spring*　　*song*　　*quarter*
*quit*　　*sung*　　*king*　　*quilt*
*quick*　　*drink*　　*bring*　　*ankle*
*queen*　　*thank*　　*pink*　　*jungle*

# Practice

**Ⓐ** Write the **New** word to complete each sentence. The **New** word will rhyme with the underlined word.

1. See the <u>ring</u> on that strange ____.   thing
2. He was crowned <u>king</u> last ____.
3. <u>Frank</u> said, "I ____ you."
4. Jane's dress is <u>pink</u>, I ____.
5. A flag <u>hung</u> as a song was ____.
6. In just a <u>bit</u>, you must ____.
7. The little <u>mink</u> took a ____.
8. They were <u>seen</u> with the ____.
9. The <u>trick</u> is to be very ____.
10. Ann likes to <u>sing</u> on the ____.

**Ⓑ** Name each picture. Write the **Review** word with the same beginning sound.

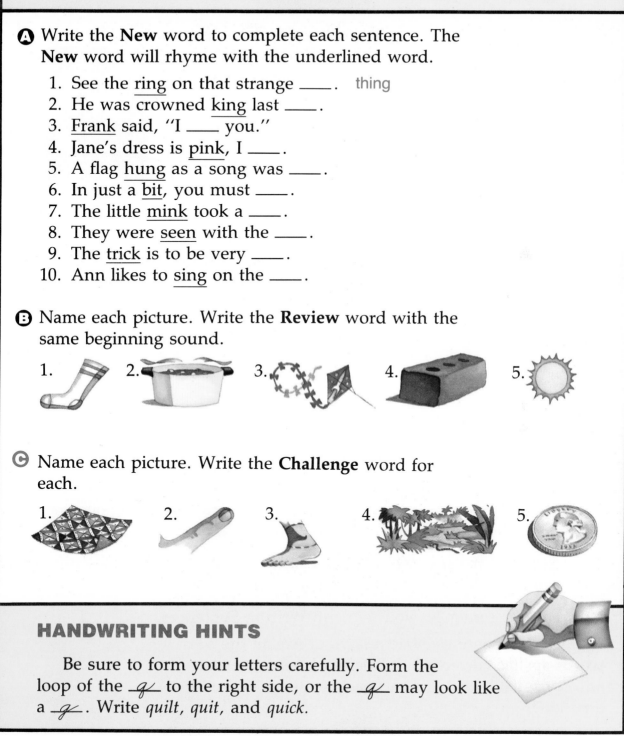

1.   2.   3.   4.   5.

**Ⓒ** Name each picture. Write the **Challenge** word for each.

1.   2.   3.   4.   5.

## HANDWRITING HINTS

Be sure to form your letters carefully. Form the loop of the _q_ to the right side, or the _q_ may look like a _g_. Write *quilt*, *quit*, and *quick*.

# Spelling and Writing: Facts

A *fact* gives information that is true. Facts can be
checked. Dictionaries and encyclopedias give facts.
Read the following facts about George Washington.

George Washington was a farmer.
George Washington was our first president.

# Writing Sentences

Read the topics on the right. Think of one fact about
each topic. You may use books to check your facts.
Write the fact in a sentence. In each sentence, use one
list word such as *spring* or *drink*.

Topics
1. spring
2. water

# Editing sentences

Choose the sentence that states a fact.
Write it correctly.

∧ add
✄ take out
= make a capital letter

1. a. Dogs are the nicest animals.
   b. dogs are are mammals.

2. a. Spring is the first seasson of the year
   b. Spring is the best seeson of all.

Now edit the sentences you wrote in **Writing Sentences.**

☐ Does each sentence state a fact? ☐ Are all the
words spelled correctly? ☐ Does each sentence start
with a capital letter? ☐ Does each sentence end with
a period?

# Review

Write the **New, Review,** and **Challenge** words that complete the chart.

| /**ng**/ spelled **ng** | | /**ng**/ spelled **n** | /**kw**/ spelled **qu** |
|---|---|---|---|
| Ⓐ | | Ⓐ | Ⓐ |
| | | | |
| | | | |
| | Ⓒ | Ⓑ | Ⓒ |
| Ⓑ | | Ⓒ | |

# Word Building

Sometimes knowing how to spell one word can help you spell other words. This is because many words may have the same *spelling pattern*. For example, the letters *-ung* are a spelling pattern. If you can spell *sung*, you may figure out how to spell *stung*. If you can spell *think*, with the pattern *-ink*, you may spell *drink*.

Add *-ung* or *-ink* to the letters below. Write the new words.

**-ung**   1. h____   hung    2. sw____    3. r____    4. cl____

**-ink**    5. s____   sink    6. bl____    7. w____    8. st____

# Content Words

You may use these /**ng**/ and /**kw**/ words in your science class.

**quart   sink   lung**

Write the word to complete each sentence. Use the Spelling Dictionary for help.

1. A metal washbowl is a ____.
2. A part of the body is the ____.
3. Two pints make up a ____.

Some words are often misspelled because they are not spelled the way they sound. That is why we must study these words carefully.

**A NEW**

was
school
about
course
friend
says
some
little
any
dear

**B REVIEW**

come
does
done
were
have

**C CHALLENGE**

again
usual
once
April
enough

Write the word that matches each clue.

**A**
1. well liked
2. used to be
3. person you like
4. group of lessons
5. whichever one
6. place to learn
7. tiny
8. few
9. speaks
10. nearly

**B**
1. ended
2. I do, you do, he ____
3. to arrive
4. I was, we ____
5. to own

**C**
1. common
2. fourth month
3. over
4. one time only
5. as much as needed

**═══ HANDWRITING MODELS ═══**

• *was*     *says*     • *come*     • *again*
*school*     *some*     *does*     *usual*
*about*     *little*     *done*     *once*
*course*     *any*     *were*     *April*
*friend*     *dear*     *have*     *enough*

# Practice

**A** Write a **New** word to complete each sentence.

1. I am taking a ＿＿ in science.
2. John was too ＿＿ for that ride.
3. We start ＿＿ in September.
4. David is my very best ＿＿ .
5. Ann is a ＿＿ friend.
6. Yesterday ＿＿ the last day.
7. I'll tell you all ＿＿ it.
8. Dad ＿＿ that we should go.
9. We would like ＿＿ cheese.
10. Jim did not drink ＿＿ milk.

**B** Write a **Review** word to complete each sentence.

1. Maria ＿＿ not know.
2. I do not ＿＿ the book.
3. Where ＿＿ you yesterday?
4. Rita will ＿＿ when she can.
5. When will the roast be ＿＿?

**C** What letters are missing? Write the **Challenge** word.

1. _pr_l      2. _g__n      3. _nc_

4. _s__l      5. _n_ _gh

---

## HANDWRITING HINTS

Be sure to form your letters carefully. If the oval
on a _d_ is not closed, the _d_ may look like the letters
_cl_. Write *dear*, *does*, and *done*.

# Spelling and Writing: Opinions

An *opinion* tells what people think or feel. An opinion cannot be checked. It is not a fact. Read the following opinions about sports.

Tennis is more fun than basketball.
It is easy to bat a baseball.

# Writing Sentences

Read the topics on the right. Think of one opinion about each topic. Write the opinion in a sentence. In each sentence, use one list word, such as *friend, little,* or *was*.

Topics
1. friends
2. games
3. school

# Editing sentences

Choose the sentence that states an opinion.
Write it correctly on the line.

1. a. Some birds build nests in trees.
   b. The bok about birds was god.

2. a. Eggs come from chickens.
   b. eggs are beter than any other food.

≡ make a capital letter
take out
∧ add

Now edit the sentences you wrote in **Writing Sentences.**
□ Does each sentence state an opinion? □ Are all the words spelled correctly? □ Does each sentence start with a capital letter? □ Does each sentence end with a period?

# Review

What letters are missing? Write each word.

**A**
1. d__r
2. w_s
3. sch__l
4. _ny
5. l_ttl_
6. s_m_
7. s_ys
8. fr__nd
9. c__rs_
10. _b__t

**B**
1. h_v_
2. d_n_
3. c_m_
4. d__s
5. w_r_

**C**
1. _s__l
2. _nc_
3. _g__n
4. _pr_l
5. _n__gh

# Dictionary Skills

*Guide words* tell the first and the last words on a dictionary page. Read this part of a dictionary page. Write the answer to each question.

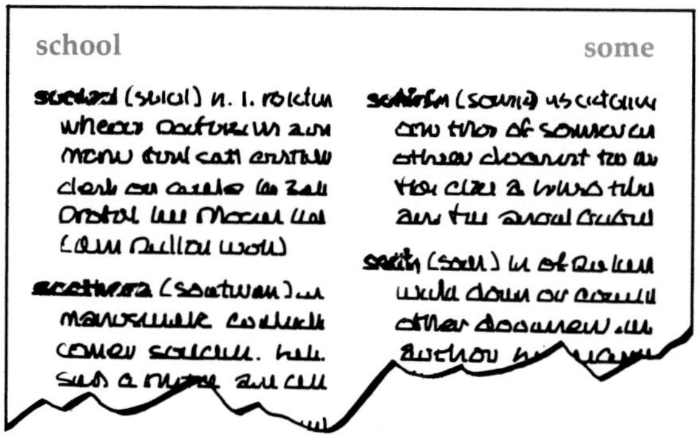

1. What is the first word on the page?
2. What is the last word on the page?
3. Is the word *say* before or after this page?
4. Is the word *such* before or after this page?

**school**        **some**

*(illustration of a dictionary page with illegible handwritten-style entries)*

# Content Words

You may use these words in your social studies class.

**captain**     **village**     **travel**

Write the word for the underlined words. Use the Spelling Dictionary for help.

1. The small <u>group of houses</u> was in the country.
2. The <u>leader of the group</u> sailed the boat.
3. They will <u>take a trip</u> to another country.

# WORDS OFTEN CONFUSED

**A NEW**

whole
hole
break
brake
knew
new
know
no
to
too
two

**B REVIEW**

our
hour
here
hear

**C CHALLENGE**

lose
loose
where
wear
we're

Some words sound the same, but they have different spellings and different meanings.

Think about the spelling and meaning of each word. Then write the correct word for each clue.

**A** 1. pair of
2. complete
3. to snap apart
4. understood
5. not at all
6. also
7. opening
8. in the direction of
9. to understand
10. not used
11. to stop

**B** 1. my, your, _____
2. in this place
3. to listen
4. time of day

**C** 1. we are
2. to be without
3. at what place
4. to put on
5. not tight

## ▌▌ HANDWRITING MODELS ▐▐

• *whole*    *new*    *two*    • *lose*
  *hole*    *know*    • *our*    *loose*
  *break*    *no*    *hour*    *where*
  *brake*    *to*    *here*    *wear*
  *knew*    *too*    *hear*    *we're*

# Practice

**Ⓐ** Write the **New** word to complete each sentence.

1. The glass will ____ if you drop it.
2. The car won't stop without a ____ .
3. I don't ____ how to do it.
4. He has ____ more than three left.
5. One and one more are ____ .
6. Carl will sing ____ .
7. I'm going ____ school.
8. There is a ____ in his shirt.
9. Kathy ate the ____ sandwich.
10. Ann ____ how it was done.
11. Pam has a ____ baby sister.

**Ⓑ** Write the **Review** words to complete each sentence.

_(1)_ friends will arrive in an _(2)_ .
Did you _(3)_ it over _(4)_ ?

**Ⓒ** Write the **Challenge** words to complete each sentence.

Sew on your l_(1)_ button so that you do not
l_(2)_ it. W_(3)_ is the dress I want to w_(4)_ to the
museum w_(5)_ going to visit.

---

## HANDWRITING HINTS

Be sure to form your letters carefully. Make the
letter _ℓ_ sit on the baseline. If it goes below the line,
it may look like an _ℓ_. Write *break* and *brake*.

# Spelling and Writing: Facts and Opinions

An *ad* tells you about things you can buy. You may have seen ads on TV or in newspapers. Some ads state facts. A *fact* gives information that is true. This ad states a fact.

Nut Muffins have whole peanuts.

Some ads state opinions. An *opinion* tells what people think or feel. This ad states an opinion.

Nut Muffins are delicious!

## Writing An Ad

Think about an ad for the Color Markers shown in the picture. Write a sentence that states a fact about the Color Markers. Then write a sentence that states an opinion about the Color Markers. In each sentence, use one list word such as *no* or *new*.

## Editing sentences

Look at the special editing symbols. Use them to correct the sentences. Write each sentence correctly. Then write **Fact** if the sentence states a fact. Write **Opinion** if the sentence states an opinion.

1. color markers are the best!
2. Six marckers are inn each set

| | |
|---|---|
| ∧ | add |
| ℘ | take out |
| ≡ | make a capital letter |

Now edit the ad you wrote in **Writing An Ad.**

☐ Does each sentence state a fact or opinion? ☐ Are all the words spelled correctly?

# Review

What letters are missing? Complete each **New**, **Review**, and **Challenge** word. Write the word.

**A** 1. n_
2. wh_l_
3. br__k
4. kn_w
5. t_
6. t__
7. kn_w
8. h_l_
9. br_k_
10. n_w
11. tw_

**B** 1. __r
2. h__r
3. h_r_
4. h__r

**C** 1. w__r
2. wh_r_
3. w_'r_
4. l__s_
5. l_s_

# Dictionary Skills

Some words sound alike but have different spellings and meanings. For example, *brake* and *break* sound alike but are spelled differently. They also have different meanings. To make sure you use the right word in a sentence, use a dictionary to check the spelling and meaning of each word. Read these words from a dictionary.

Write the word that completes each sentence.

1. Be careful not to ____ the glass.
2. Dad stopped the sled with a ____ .
3. Please leave the book ____ .
4. I will speak louder if you cannot ____ me.

> **brake** /brāk/ *n.* something used to stop.
> **break** /brāk/ *v.* to make into pieces.
>
> **hear** /hir/ *v.* to listen to sound.
> **here** /hir/ *adv.* in this place.

# Content Words

You may use these words in your reading class.

**in  inn  steak  stake**

Write the words to complete each sentence. Use the Spelling Dictionary for help.

He owns an __(1)__ that is __(2)__ the country.
He roasted the __(3)__ on a __(4)__ over the fire.

# UNIT 24  REVIEW: UNITS 19-23

/n/ is spelled **kn**; /r/ is spelled **wr**
/m/ is spelled **mb**; /f/ is spelled **lf**

| | | | | |
|---|---|---|---|---|
| half | knew | write | knot | lamb |
| wrap | climb | calf | knock | knit |

1. Write the words that begin with two consonants.
2. Write the words that end with two consonants.
3. Write the words that begin and end with two consonants.

/ch/ is spelled **ch**; /th/ is spelled **th**
/hw/ is spelled **wh**; /sh/ is spelled **sh**

| | | | | |
|---|---|---|---|---|
| while | path | which | three | they |
| much | child | wish | with | ship |

Read the clues. Write a word for each. The word in the box gives the answer to this riddle.

**Riddle:** What do you call time on your hands?

1. want very much
2. one, two, ____, four
3. at the same time as
4. send by boat, train, or truck
5. I, you, he, she, we, ____
6. what one
7. track
8. by the use of
9. young boy or girl
10. great deal

# UNIT 21

/**ng**/ is spelled **ng** or **n**; /**kw**/ is spelled **qu**

| | | | | |
|---|---|---|---|---|
| think | swing | quit | quick | queen |
| thing | spring | sung | drink | thank |

A. Find the words that begin with an **s**. Then write them in ABC order.

1. ___  2. ___  3. ___

B. Find the words that begin with the /**th**/ sound. Then write each one.

4. ___  5. ___  6. ___

C. Read each clue. Write the word for each clue.

7. to swallow water  9. fast
8. to stop  10. king's wife

# UNIT 22

Some words are misspelled because they are not spelled the way they sound.

| | | | | |
|---|---|---|---|---|
| was | school | about | course | friend |
| says | some | little | any | dear |

Solve the puzzle. Write the word for each clue.

**Across**
1. they were, I ___
4. nearly
5. person you enjoy
7. a number of things
8. tiny
9. some

**Down**
2. place to learn
3. group of classes or lessons
6. nice, well liked
7. speaks

Some words sound the same, but they have different spellings and different meanings.

| whole | hole | break | brake | knew | new |
|-------|------|-------|-------|------|-----|
| know  | no   | to    | too   | two  |     |

Choose the correct word for each blank. Write the word.

I will take _(1)_ friends _(2)_ the movies _(3)_ .
He _(4)_ very well that the shirt was _(5)_ .
There was not one _(6)_ in the _(7)_ piece.
There is _(8)_ way to _(9)_ how old he is.
There must be a _(10)_ somewhere because the _(11)_ does not work.

# Word Building

Add the beginning or ending to each word. Write the whole word.

1. The sailor (knot + ed) the rope.   knotted
2. The children (un + wrap) their presents.
3. Joel (wish + es) for a new bicycle.
4. The students (re + write) their stories.
5. Grandma is (knit + ing) a cap.
6. The girls are (write + ing) about their trip.
7. This new bed is very (spring + y).
8. My dog is a faster (drink + er) than yours.
9. Which of the three (path + s) is best?
10. My brother (thank + ed) me for my help.

Read each set of words. Mark the word that is misspelled. If none of the words in the set is misspelled, mark **none** ⓓ.

1. ⓐ hafe
   ⓑ while
   ⓒ think
   ⓓ none

2. ⓐ whole
   ⓑ wus
   ⓒ knew
   ⓓ none

3. ⓐ path
   ⓑ swing
   ⓒ skool
   ⓓ none

4. ⓐ hole
   ⓑ write
   ⓒ which
   ⓓ none

5. ⓐ about
   ⓑ qwit
   ⓒ break
   ⓓ none

6. ⓐ knot
   ⓑ three
   ⓒ quick
   ⓓ none

7. ⓐ course
   ⓑ break
   ⓒ lam
   ⓓ none

8. ⓐ frend
   ⓑ they
   ⓒ queen
   ⓓ none

9. ⓐ knew
   ⓑ wrap
   ⓒ much
   ⓓ none

10. ⓐ thing
    ⓑ seys
    ⓒ new
    ⓓ none

11. ⓐ clime
    ⓑ child
    ⓒ spring
    ⓓ none

12. ⓐ some
    ⓑ know
    ⓒ calf
    ⓓ none

13. ⓐ wish
    ⓑ sung
    ⓒ littel
    ⓓ none

14. ⓐ knok
    ⓑ no
    ⓒ with
    ⓓ none

15. ⓐ drink
    ⓑ eny
    ⓒ to
    ⓓ none

16. ⓐ knit
    ⓑ ship
    ⓒ thank
    ⓓ none

17. ⓐ dear
    ⓑ too
    ⓒ two
    ⓓ none

18. ⓐ says
    ⓑ brake
    ⓒ break
    ⓓ none

19. ⓐ lamb
    ⓑ half
    ⓒ thay
    ⓓ none

20. ⓐ hole
    ⓑ drik
    ⓒ path
    ⓓ none

21. ⓐ spring
    ⓑ caf
    ⓒ new
    ⓓ none

22. ⓐ swing
    ⓑ to
    ⓒ whith
    ⓓ none

23. ⓐ knew
    ⓑ wile
    ⓒ not
    ⓓ none

24. ⓐ rite
    ⓑ course
    ⓒ some
    ⓓ none

# 25

# THE /är/ and /ôr/ SOUNDS

## A NEW

store

sore

arm

art

storm

or

start

large

born

sport

## B REVIEW

part

car

dark

hard

far

## C CHALLENGE

fourth

normal

forth

order

board

/är/ is spelled **ar** as in *jar*
/ôr/ is spelled **or** as in *morning*
**ore** as in *shore*

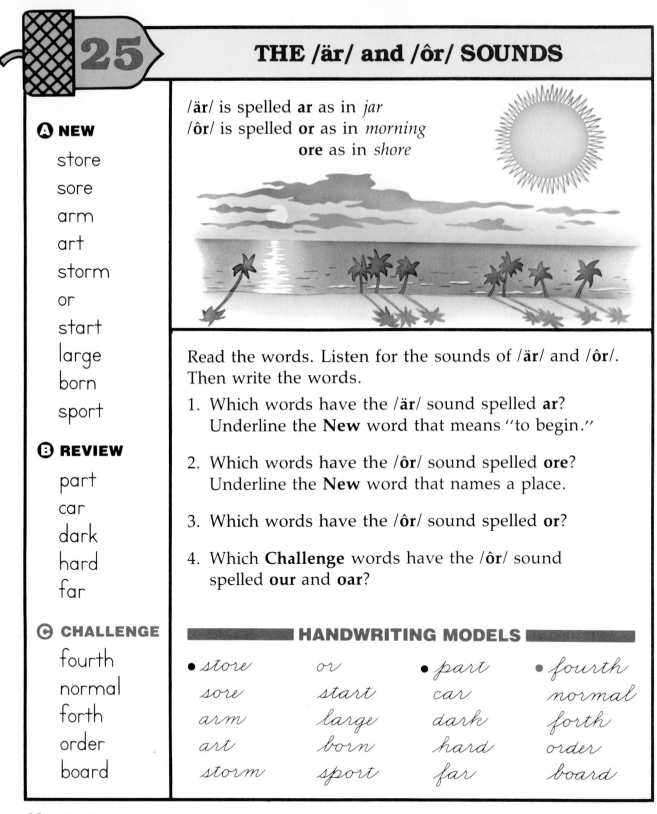

Read the words. Listen for the sounds of /**är**/ and /**ôr**/. Then write the words.

1. Which words have the /**är**/ sound spelled **ar**? Underline the **New** word that means "to begin."

2. Which words have the /**ôr**/ sound spelled **ore**? Underline the **New** word that names a place.

3. Which words have the /**ôr**/ sound spelled **or**?

4. Which **Challenge** words have the /**ôr**/ sound spelled **our** and **oar**?

### HANDWRITING MODELS

• *store*  *or*  • *part*  • *fourth*
*sore*  *start*  *car*  *normal*
*arm*  *large*  *dark*  *forth*
*art*  *born*  *hard*  *order*
*storm*  *sport*  *far*  *board*

# Practice

**A** Write a **New** word to complete each sentence.

1. Baseball is my favorite ____.
2. Inés buys milk at the corner ____.
3. Anita fell and now her knee is ____.
4. Last night my new sister was ____.
5. Mandy's bag was on her right ____.
6. There was a bad ____ last night.
7. Rosa saw art at the ____ museum.
8. Do it either now ____ or later.
9. The race is about to ____.
10. The elephant is a ____ animal.

**B** Name each picture. Write the **Review** word with the same beginning sound.

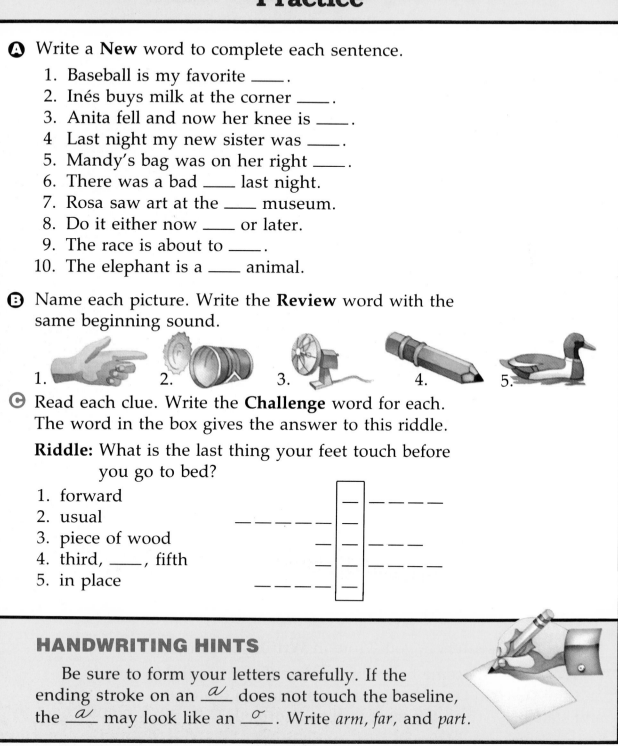

1.    2.    3.    4.    5.

**C** Read each clue. Write the **Challenge** word for each. The word in the box gives the answer to this riddle.

**Riddle:** What is the last thing your feet touch before you go to bed?

1. forward    — — — — — —
2. usual    — — — — — — —
3. piece of wood    — — — — —
4. third, ____, fifth    — — — — —
5. in place    — — — — — —

## HANDWRITING HINTS

   Be sure to form your letters carefully. If the ending stroke on an _a_ does not touch the baseline, the _a_ may look like an _o_. Write *arm*, *far*, and *part*.

# Spelling and Writing: Commas

Use a *comma* (,) between the name of the city and the state.

　　We travel to Sante Fe, New Mexico.

Use a *comma* (,) between the day of the month and the year.

　　They visit the museum on August 15, 1982.

# Writing Sentences

Write two sentences that tell about a trip to a special city. Write the name of the city and state in one sentence. Write the date and year in the other sentence. Use commas when necessary. In each sentence, use one list word such as *large* or *start*.

# Editing sentences

Look at the special editing symbols. Use them to correct the sentences. Write each sentence correctly.

| ⌃ add comma |
| ⌀ take out |

1. The art show is in in Dallas Texas.

2. I hurt my arm on May 3 1982.

3. The storm was on June 1 1982.

Now edit the sentences you wrote in **Writing Sentences.**

☐ Does a comma come between the day of the month and the year? ☐ Does a comma come between the city and state? ☐ Are all the words spelled correctly?

# Review

What letters are missing? Complete each **New, Review,** and **Challenge** word. Write the word.

**A** 1. sp__t
2. l__ge
3. _r
4. __t
5. s___

6. st___
7. __m
8. st__m
9. st__t
10. b__n

**B** 1. f__
2. d__k
3. p__t
4. h__d
5. c__

**C** 1. b___d
2. f__th
3. f___th
4. __der
5. n__mal

# Word Building

Sometimes knowing how to spell one word can help you spell other words. This is because many words may have the same *spelling pattern*. For example, the letters *-ore* are a spelling pattern. If you can spell *sore*, you may figure out how to spell *store*. If you can spell *car*, which has the pattern *-ar*, you may figure out how to spell *far*.

Add *-ore* or *-ar* to the letters below. Write the words.

**-ore** 1. m____ more    2. t____    3. sh____    4. w____

**-ar** 5. b____ bar    6. t____    7. st____    8. j____

# Content Words

You may use these /är/ and /ôr/ words in your social studies class.

    **orchard**     **harbor**     **border**

Write the word to complete each sentence. Use the Spelling Dictionary for help.

1. He lives near the ____ of the two states.
2. Our farm has an apple ____.
3. The ship sailed into the ____.

# 26

# THE /ėr/ SOUND

/ėr/ is spelled **er** as in *herd*
          **ur** as in *spur*
          **ir** as in *shirt*

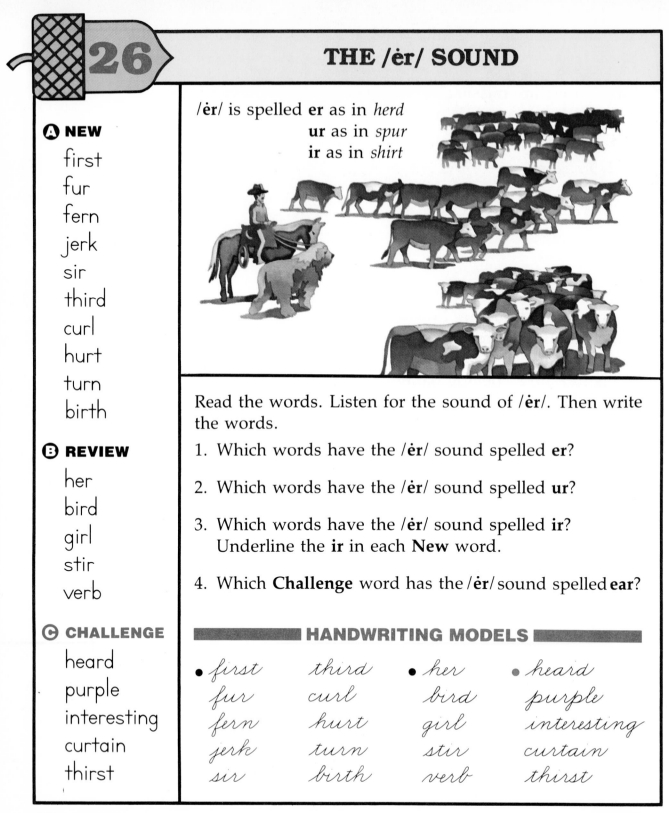

**A NEW**

first
fur
fern
jerk
sir
third
curl
hurt
turn
birth

**B REVIEW**

her
bird
girl
stir
verb

**C CHALLENGE**

heard
purple
interesting
curtain
thirst

Read the words. Listen for the sound of /ėr/. Then write the words.

1. Which words have the /ėr/ sound spelled **er**?

2. Which words have the /ėr/ sound spelled **ur**?

3. Which words have the /ėr/ sound spelled **ir**? Underline the **ir** in each **New** word.

4. Which **Challenge** word has the /ėr/ sound spelled **ear**?

## HANDWRITING MODELS

• first      third      • her       • heard
  fur        curl        bird        purple
  fern       hurt        girl        interesting
  jerk       turn        stir        curtain
  sir        birth       verb        thirst

# Practice

**A** Write the **New** word to complete each sentence.

1. Bob had to twist and ___ his hand away.
2. Susan bought a coat of ___ .
3. Luisa wants to be the last one in line, not the ___ .
4. My mother has a ___ growing in the garden.
5. If you are not careful, you could get ___ .
6. Now it is my ___ to ride the bike.
7. Her hair is so straight that Kim has to ___ it.
8. Jack was first, Kevin was second, and I was ___ .
9. July 14, 1975 is her date of ___ .
10. The waiter said to the man, "May I help you, ___ ?"

**B** Write the **Review** words in ABC order.

**C** Write the **Challenge** word with the same ending.

1. ap**ple**
2. moun**tain**
3. thi**rd**
4. fi**rst**
5. k**ing**

## HANDWRITING HINTS

Be sure to form your letters carefully. If the letter _u_ is not left open at the top, the _u_ may look like an _a_ . Write *fur, curl,* and *hurt.*

## Spelling and Writing: Capitals and Periods

Use a *capital letter* to begin the first word in a sentence.

The third player hits a home run.

Use a *period* (.) at the end of a sentence that makes a statement.

Suzy runs to first base.

Use a *question mark* (?) at the end of a sentence that asks something.

Did a player get hurt?

Use an *exclamation mark* (!) at the end of a sentence that shows strong feeling or excitement.

What a good game that was!

# Writing Sentences

Think about a game of baseball. Write three sentences about the game. Have one sentence make a statement. Have another sentence ask a question. Have another sentence show excitement. In each sentence, use a list word, such as *turn, third,* or *first.*

| | |
|---|---|
| ≡ | make a capital letter |
| ∧ | add |
| ℒ | take out |

# Editin^g sentencess

Look at the special editing symbols. Use them to correct the sentences. Write each sentence correctly.

1. i curl my hand around bat.    2. how fasst the first game went

Now edit the sentences you wrote in **Writing Sentences.**

☐ Does each sentence begin with a capital letter?
☐ Does each sentence end with correct punctuation?
☐ Are all the words spelled correctly?

# Review

What letters are missing? Complete each **New, Review,** and **Challenge** word. Write the word.

**Ⓐ** 1. b__th
2. h__t
3. th__d
4. j__k
5. f__

6. f__st
7. f__n
8. s__
9. c__l
10. t__n

**Ⓑ** 1. v__b
2. g__l
3. h__
4. b__d
5. st__

**Ⓒ** 1. int__esting
2. h___d
3. th__st
4. c__tain
5. p__ple

# Dictionary Skills

Suppose you needed to spell a word with /ėr/, like

How can you find the spelling? Write the ways to spell /ėr/.

1. /ėr/ can be spelled __
2. /ėr/ can be spelled __
3. /ėr/ can be spelled __

Which way to spell /ėr/ is the correct way for this word?

**terkey     turkey     tirkey**

Write the correct word.
Use your Spelling Dictionary for help.

# Content Words

You may use these /ėr/ words in your social studies class.

**herd     modern     serve**

Write the word to complete each sentence. Use the Spelling Dictionary for help.

1. She will ___ as mayor for four years.
2. The cowboys will ___ and drive the cattle.
3. The rocket is a ___ invention.

# 27

# SPELLING CONTRACTIONS

## Ⓐ NEW
can't
don't
I'm
doesn't
didn't
I'll
we're
isn't
let's
there's

## Ⓑ REVIEW
she's
he's
that's
what's

## Ⓒ CHALLENGE
haven't
couldn't
won't
I've
hasn't

A *contraction* is one word made from two words. Some of the letters are left out. An *apostrophe* (')takes the place of the letters that are left out.

we will → we'll

Read each word and notice where the apostrophe is placed. Think about the two words that make up each contraction. Then write the contraction for each pair of words.

Ⓐ 1. can not
2. I am
3. I will
4. let us
5. do not
6. does not
7. did not

8. we are
9. is not
10. there is
Ⓑ 1. she is
2. he is
3. that is
4. what is

Ⓒ 1. will not
2. I have
3. has not
4. have not
5. could not

## HANDWRITING MODELS

- *can't*      *I'll*        • *she's*       • *haven't*
  *don't*      *we're*         *he's*          *couldn't*
  *I'm*        *isn't*         *that's*        *won't*
  *doesn't*    *let's*         *what's*        *I've*
  *didn't*     *there's*                       *hasn't*

# Practice

**A** Write the **New** word to complete each sentence.

1. Kathy still ____ want to go.
2. The doctor said that ____ be fine.
3. There ____ enough time to finish.
4. I ____ go with you today.
5. We ____ know where the ball is!
6. I know that ____ a book for you.
7. On Monday ____ going to school.
8. Dad said that ____ not leaving yet.
9. Pam ____ tell me what happened.
10. Al said to Joe, "Now, ____ leave."

**B** Read each word. Write the **Review** word with the same beginning sound.

1. <u>wh</u>eel    2. <u>sh</u>ell    3. <u>th</u>is    4. <u>h</u>and

**C** Write a **Challenge** word that is the opposite of each of the underlined words in each sentence.

1. Elisa <u>could</u> have gone yesterday.
2. <u>I have</u> a dime in my pocket.
3. He <u>has</u> had enough time.
4. I <u>will</u> ask father.
5. I <u>have not</u> had a chance.

## HANDWRITING HINTS

If the *apostrophe* (') in a contraction is left out, the contraction may look like another word. Write *I'll*, *we're*, and *she'll*.

## Spelling and Writing: An Introduction

An *introduction* is a way to help people meet each other. You may introduce a new friend to an old friend. In an introduction, you may tell something about the new person. Read this introduction.

I'm happy to meet you. Let's play a game together.

Thank you, Kate. There's my bat and ball. Why don't we play baseball?

I would like you to meet my new friend Robert. He doesn't live nearby. He's staying at our house.

# Writing An Introduction

Imagine that you have a new friend to introduce to your family. Write an introduction. Begin with this sentence.

*I would like you to meet my new friend _____ .*

Fill in your friend's name. Then write two sentences that tell something about the person. Use a list word in each sentence, such as *doesn't* or *isn't*.

# Editing An introduction

Look at the special editing symbols. Then edit the introduction. Use the symbols to correct the sentences. If you need to, write your introduction again.

≡ make a capital letter
∧ add
⌿ take out

☐ Does each sentence begin with a capital letter?
☐ Does each sentence end with a period? ☐ Are all words spelled correctly?

# Review

What is missing? Complete each **New, Review,** and **Challenge** word with the apostrophe in the correct place. Write the word.

**A** 1. theres
2. cant
3. lets
4. dont
5. isnt

6. Im
7. doesnt
8. were
9. Ill
10. didnt

**B** 1. whats
2. shes
3. thats
4. hes

**C** 1. hasnt
2. Ive
3. wont
4. couldnt
5. havent

# Dictionary Skills

One type of word in a dictionary is a *contraction.* Look at the following word:

**we're**    /wir/    we are

The word has its pronunciation and the two words that make up the contraction. Read each contraction. Write the two words that make up the contraction. Use your Spelling Dictionary for help.

1. you've
2. aren't

3. she'll
4. they're

# Content Words

You may use these words in your English reading.

**contraction    language    sentence**

Write the word to complete each sentence. Use the Spelling Dictionary for help.

1. Adam wants to learn a new ____ .
2. The word *they're* is a ____ .
3. Rita must write a ____ for each word.

# 28

# COMPOUND WORDS

A *compound word* is a word that is made up of two other words.

homework  →  home + work

Ⓐ **NEW**

maybe
anything
everyone
popcorn
something
anyway
driveway
schoolyard
grandmother
outside

Ⓑ **REVIEW**

cupcake
playtime
classroom
himself
inside

Ⓒ **CHALLENGE**

footstep
sometime
birthday
cannot
breakfast

Read each word. Think about the two words that make up each compound word. Then write the compound word that matches each clue.

Ⓐ 1. your mother's mother
2. road to a garage
3. perhaps
4. all persons
5. thing of any sort
6. heated burst corn
7. a certain thing
8. not indoors
9. playground
10. in any manner

Ⓑ 1. indoors
2. time to exercise
3. form of he
4. small baked cake
5. room in a school

Ⓒ 1. not able
2. step of a foot
3. day one was born
4. an unknown time
5. morning meal

■■■■■■■■■ **HANDWRITING MODELS** ■■■■■■■■

- *maybe*
  *anything*
  *everyone*
  *popcorn*
  *something*
  *anyway*
  *driveway*

  *schoolyard*
  *grandmother*
  *outside*
- *cupcake*
  *playtime*
  *classroom*
  *himself*

  *inside*
- *footstep*
  *sometime*
  *birthday*
  *cannot*
  *breakfast*

# Practice

**Ⓐ** Write the **New** word to complete each sentence.

1. Don't play ____ in the rain.
2. My ____ came to visit us.
3. The car is in the ____.
4. After lunch we play in the ____.
5. I don't have ____ to do today.
6. If we finish, then ____ we can go.
7. We ate ____ at the movies.
8. Almost ____ in the family came.
9. I don't like it, but I'll do it ____.
10. There is ____ strange outside.

**Ⓑ** Match a **List a** word with a **b** word to make a compound word. Then write the **Review** word.

|    | a     | b     |
|----|-------|-------|
| 1. | in    | cake  |
| 2. | class | side  |
| 3. | cup   | room  |
| 4. | play  | self  |
| 5. | him   | time  |

**Ⓒ** Read each clue. Write the **Challenge** word for each.

1. first meal of the day
2. sound of someone walking
3. not able to
4. day one was born
5. one day

# Word History

Some words name a sound that you hear. For example, when popcorn is heated, you hear this sound: *pop!* The word *pop* comes from the sound that you hear.

Other words that copy a sound are *zoom*, *crash*, and *buzz*. Think of another word that names a sound.

# Spelling and Writing: A Thank-You Note

You write a *thank-you note* to thank someone for something. The *date* tells when it was written. The *greeting* tells to whom it was written. The *paragraph* thanks the person for what was done. The *closing* says "good-by." The *name* tells who wrote the note.

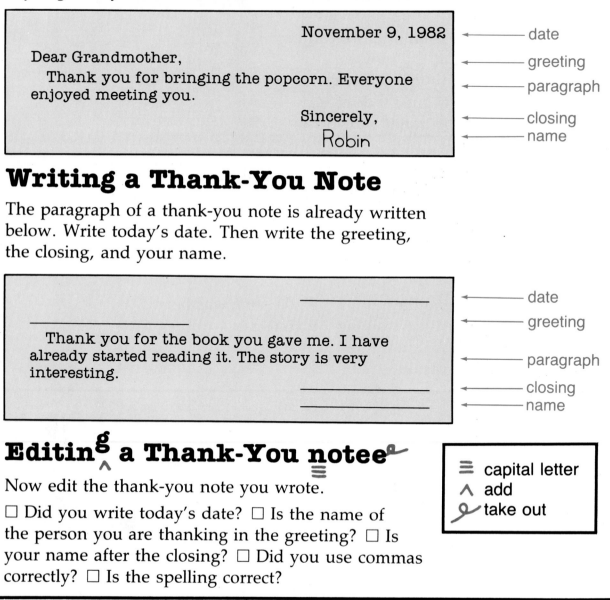

November 9, 1982 ←——— date

Dear Grandmother, ←——— greeting
    Thank you for bringing the popcorn. Everyone ←——— paragraph
enjoyed meeting you.

                    Sincerely, ←——— closing
                      Robin ←——— name

# Writing a Thank-You Note

The paragraph of a thank-you note is already written below. Write today's date. Then write the greeting, the closing, and your name.

——————————— ←——— date

———————————— ←——— greeting
    Thank you for the book you gave me. I have
already started reading it. The story is very ←——— paragraph
interesting.

                    ——————————— ←——— closing
                    ——————————— ←——— name

# Editing a Thank-You note

Now edit the thank-you note you wrote.

☐ Did you write today's date? ☐ Is the name of the person you are thanking in the greeting? ☐ Is your name after the closing? ☐ Did you use commas correctly? ☐ Is the spelling correct?

≡ capital letter
∧ add
ℓ take out

# Review

Complete each **New, Review,** and **Challenge** word.
Write the word.

**A**
1. out____
2. any____
3. may____
4. grand____
5. school____
6. every____
7. drive____
8. pop____
9. some____
10. any____

**B**
1. in____
2. play____
3. him____
4. cup____
5. class____

**C**
1. break____
2. can____
3. foot____
4. some____
5. birth____

# Word Building

The words *some* and *thing* can be joined to make the compound word *something*.

some + thing = something

Write a compound word by joining each pair of words below.

1. book + shelf   bookshelf
2. tooth + brush
3. some + where
4. oat + meal
5. rain + drop
6. over + coat

# Content Words

You may use these compound words in your social studies class.

**landform     skyline     grassland**

Write the word to complete each sentence. Use the Spelling Dictionary for help.

1. A ____ is *land* covered with *grass*.
2. A ____ is a *form* on the *land* surface.
3. A ____ is the *line* where earth and *sky* meet.

**Ⓐ NEW**

woman
because
cousin
vacation
been
women
people
use
together
please

**Ⓑ REVIEW**

said
want
that
could
uncle

**Ⓒ CHALLENGE**

tear
tired
sure
trouble
believe

Some words are often misspelled because they are not spelled the way they sound.

Write the word that matches each clue.

**Ⓐ**
1. to be so kind
2. to do something with
3. ladies
4. one with the other
5. since
6. trip
7. your aunt's child
8. was
9. men, ladies, children
10. one lady

**Ⓑ**
1. your mother's brother
2. this, ____, these, those
3. spoken
4. to wish
5. was able

**Ⓒ**
1. to think
2. to rip
3. certain
4. problem
5. sleepy

**HANDWRITING MODELS**

• *woman*        *women*        • *said*        • *tear*
  *because*        *people*        *want*        *tired*
  *cousin*        *use*        *that*        *sure*
  *vacation*        *together*        *could*        *trouble*
  *been*        *please*        *uncle*        *believe*

# Practice

**Ⓐ** Write the **New** word to complete each sentence.

1. May I ____ have a sandwich?
2. John and Elena are going ____.
3. Mom is the only ____ there.
4. Our family is going on a ____.
5. He'll do it ____ he is so nice.
6. The men and ____ cleaned up.
7. Many ____ were at the dance.
8. Where have you ____?
9. Anita will ____ it after you.
10. My uncle and my ____ played.

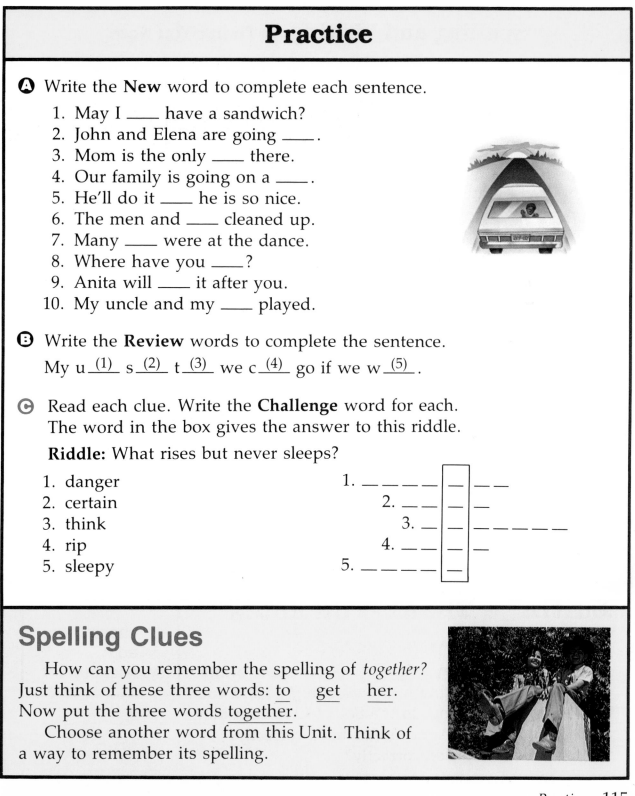

**Ⓑ** Write the **Review** words to complete the sentence.

My u _(1)_ s _(2)_ t _(3)_ we c _(4)_ go if we w _(5)_ .

**Ⓒ** Read each clue. Write the **Challenge** word for each. The word in the box gives the answer to this riddle.

**Riddle:** What rises but never sleeps?

1. danger
2. certain
3. think
4. rip
5. sleepy

1. _ _ _ _ | _ | _ _
2. _ _ | _ | _
3. _ | _ | _ _ _ _ _
4. _ _ | _ | _
5. _ _ _ _ | _

## Spelling Clues

How can you remember the spelling of *together?* Just think of these three words: to   get   her. Now put the three words together.

Choose another word from this Unit. Think of a way to remember its spelling.

# Spelling and Writing: A Thank-You Note

You write a *thank-you note* to thank someone for something. The *date* tells when it was written. The *greeting* tells to whom it was written. The *paragraph* thanks the person for what was

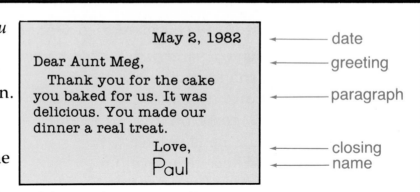

May 2, 1982 ← date

Dear Aunt Meg, ← greeting

Thank you for the cake you baked for us. It was delicious. You made our dinner a real treat. ← paragraph

Love, ← closing
Paul ← name

done. The *closing* says "good-by." The *name* tells who wrote the note.

# Writing A Thank-You Note

Pretend that you have visited cousins on a ranch. Write them a thank-you note. Use the form below. In each sentence, use one list word such as *vacation, together,* or *people.*

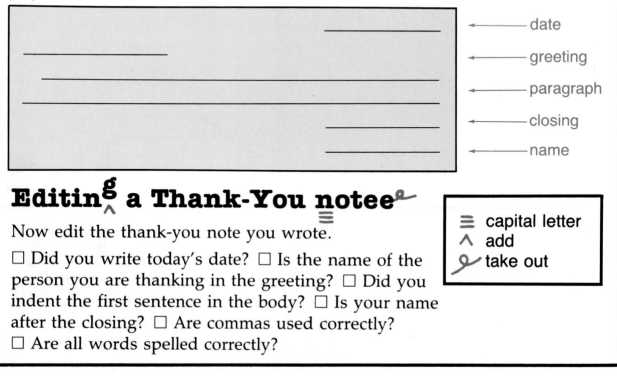

← date

← greeting

← paragraph

← closing

← name

# Editing a Thank-You notee

Now edit the thank-you note you wrote.

☐ Did you write today's date? ☐ Is the name of the person you are thanking in the greeting? ☐ Did you indent the first sentence in the body? ☐ Is your name after the closing? ☐ Are commas used correctly?
☐ Are all words spelled correctly?

| ≡ capital letter |
| ∧ add |
| ℘ take out |

# Review

What letters are missing? Complete each **New, Review,** and **Challenge** word. Write the word.

**Ⓐ**
1. w_men
2. w_m_n
3. pl__s_
4. _s_
5. t_g_th_r
6. p__pl_
7. b_c__s_
8. c__s_n
9. v_c_t__n
10. b__n

**Ⓑ**
1. _ncl_
2. c__ld
3. w_nt
4. th_t
5. s__d

**Ⓒ**
1. s_r_
2. tr__bl_
3. t__r
4. b_l__v_
5. t_r_d

# Word Building

Often several words belong to a *word family*. Recognizing a word family can help you spell a particular word. For example, suppose you were unsure whether the spelling of *pleasure* is *pleashure, pleazure,* or *pleasure*. Think of another word in the same family: *please.* If you know that *please* has an *s,* you may figure out that *pleasure* is also spelled with an *s.*

Write each word completely.

1. plea_e    please
2. plea_ant
3. plea_ure
4. plea_ing

# Content Words

You may use these words in your science class.

**blossom    camera    electric**

Write the word to complete each sentence. Use the Spelling Dictionary for help.

1. A white ___ fell from the tree.
2. Children enjoy watching ___ trains.
3. People can take pictures with a ___.

# UNIT 30 REVIEW: UNITS 25-29

## UNIT 25

/är/ is spelled **ar**; /ôr/ is spelled **or** or **ore**

| | | | | |
|---|---|---|---|---|
| store | sore | arm | art | storm |
| or | start | large | born | sport |

Read each clue. Write the word to complete the puzzle.

**Across**
2. feel hurt
3. begin
4. either, ____
6. your hand is part of the ____
8. place to buy goods
9. painting, dance, or music

**Down**
1. brought into life
2. rainy or snowy weather
5. huge
7. game

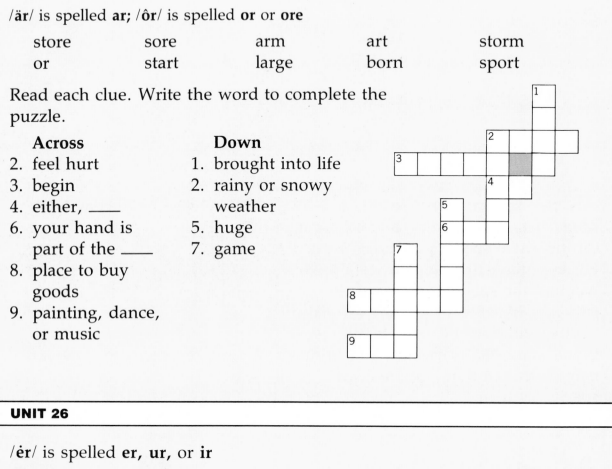

## UNIT 26

/er/ is spelled **er, ur,** or **ir**

| | | | | |
|---|---|---|---|---|
| first | third | fur | fern | jerk |
| sir | curl | hurt | turn | birth |

Write the word that ends the same way as each word.

1. wo<u>rk</u>
2. ca<u>rt</u>
3. wo<u>rth</u>
4. he<u>r</u>
5. ca<u>r</u>
6. bu<u>rn</u>
7. lea<u>rn</u>
8. bu<u>rst</u>
9. ca<u>rd</u>
10. swi<u>rl</u>

A **contraction** is a word made from two words. Some
of the letters are left out. An **apostrophe** takes the place
of the letter or letters that are left out in a contraction.

| | | | | |
|---|---|---|---|---|
| can't | don't | I'm | doesn't | didn't |
| I'll | we're | isn't | let's | there's |

Write the contraction for the underlined words
in each sentence.

1. I <u>do not</u> want to go.
2. Jane <u>did not</u> eat her lunch.
3. We hope <u>there is</u> a chance.
4. Mike <u>can not</u> run that far.
5. <u>I am</u> leaving tomorrow.
6. Mary <u>is not</u> going.
7. Jim <u>does not</u> know how.
8. Rita said, "Now, <u>let us</u> begin."
9. <u>I will</u> write Pat a letter.
10. Later on <u>we are</u> going to sing.

A **compound word** is a word that is made up of two
other words.

| | | | | |
|---|---|---|---|---|
| maybe | anything | something | everyone | popcorn |
| anyway | driveway | schoolyard | grandmother | outside |

Match a word from **List a** with a word from **List b** to
make a compound word. Write each word.

| | a | b |
|---|---|---|
| 1. | out | thing |
| 2. | may | one |
| 3. | pop | way |
| 4. | some | yard |
| 5. | school | mother |
| 6. | any | be |
| 7. | grand | side |
| 8. | drive | thing |
| 9. | any | way |
| 10. | every | corn |

Some words are spelled differently than they sound.

| women | because | cousin | vacation | been |
|-------|---------|--------|----------|------|
| woman | people | together | use | please |

Read each clue. Write the word for each clue.

1. make happy
2. more than one lady
3. take often
4. one with the other
5. persons
6. one lady
7. was
8. trip
9. since
10. child of an aunt

## Word Building

Add the beginning or ending to each word. Write the complete word.

1. The farmer is (store + ing) food now.   storing
2. The evening was very (storm + y).
3. We cut the grass around four (driveway + s).
4. Mother (use + ed) a large pan for baking.
5. The (burn + er) on the stove is broken.
6. The animals were (un + hurt) by the storm.
7. The family took two (vacation + s).
8. My gift (please + ed) my little brother.
9. No one is (use + ing) the telephone now.
10. Today is Mike's (birth + day).

Complete each sentence. Mark the word that is spelled correctly.

1. His arm is very ____.    ⓐ soar    **ⓑ** sore
2. Jane will either go now ____ later.    ⓐ or    ⓑ oar
3. The cat's ____ is very soft.    ⓐ fir    ⓑ fur
4. Now it's my ____ to jump.    ⓐ tern    ⓑ turn
5. I think ____ leave now.    ⓐ Ill    ⓑ I'll
6. Next week ____ going home.    ⓐ we're    ⓑ were
7. Where have you ____?    ⓐ bin    ⓑ been
8. What is your date of ____?    ⓐ birth    ⓑ berth
9. Be sure to ____ your pen.    ⓐ use    ⓑ us
10. When were you ____?    ⓐ borne    ⓑ born

Read each group of words. Mark the word that is misspelled.

11. store ⓐ
    furst **ⓑ**
    maybe ⓒ

12. wuman ⓐ
    don't ⓑ
    anything ⓒ

13. because ⓐ
    arm ⓑ
    firn ⓒ

14. Im ⓐ
    everyone ⓑ
    cousin ⓒ

15. art ⓐ
    jurk ⓑ
    doesn't ⓒ

16. vacashun ⓐ
    popcorn ⓑ
    storm ⓒ

17. anyway ⓐ
    thurd ⓑ
    start ⓒ

18. didn't ⓐ
    something ⓑ
    sur ⓒ

19. wimen ⓐ
    curl ⓑ
    driveway ⓒ

20. large ⓐ
    hurt ⓑ
    peeple ⓒ

21. use ⓐ
    we're ⓑ
    maybee ⓒ

22. grandmother ⓐ
    tugether ⓑ
    there's ⓒ

23. can't ⓐ
    sport ⓑ
    owtside ⓒ

24. sore ⓐ
    pleese ⓑ
    fur ⓒ

25. been ⓐ
    or ⓑ
    dont ⓒ

26. schoolyard ⓐ
    isnt ⓑ
    let's ⓒ

# WORDS WITH DOUBLE CONSONANTS

**A NEW**

balloon
hello
happen
suppose
lesson
button
bottom
ribbon
mitten
sudden

**B REVIEW**

yellow
apple
arrow
hidden
kitten

**C CHALLENGE**

slippery
manner
collar
attic
different

Many two-syllable words have double consonants in the middle. The double consonants have only one sound.

Read the words. Listen for the middle consonant sound. Write each word. Underline the double consonant letters.

**A** 1. -dd-          2. -pp-          3. -pp-

4. -bb-          5. -ss-          6. -ll-

7. -ll-          8. -tt-          9. -tt-

10. -tt-     **B** 1. -dd-          2. -tt-

3. -rr-          4. -pp-          5. -ll-

**C** 1. -ll-          2. -tt-          3. -nn-

4. -pp-          5. -ff-

═══ **HANDWRITING MODELS** ═══

- *balloon*     *button*     • *yellow*     • *slippery*
  *hello*       *bottom*       *apple*        *manner*
  *happen*      *ribbon*       *arrow*        *collar*
  *suppose*     *mitten*       *hidden*       *attic*
  *lesson*      *sudden*       *kitten*       *different*

# Practice

**A** Write a **New** word to complete each sentence.

1. All of a ___ it fell down.
2. What do you ___ happened?
3. She wore a ___ in her hair.
4. Please sew on the loose ___.
5. What will ___ next?
6. She said ___ to me.
7. Jane put the ___ on her hand.
8. Carlos blew up the ___ for me.
9. It was at the ___ of the bag.
10. I did the fourth ___ at home.

**B** Read each clue. Write the **Review** word for each.
The word in the box gives the answer to this riddle.

**Riddle:** What do friendly bees call each other?

1. covered up
2. pointed wood
3. young cat
4. fruit
5. light color

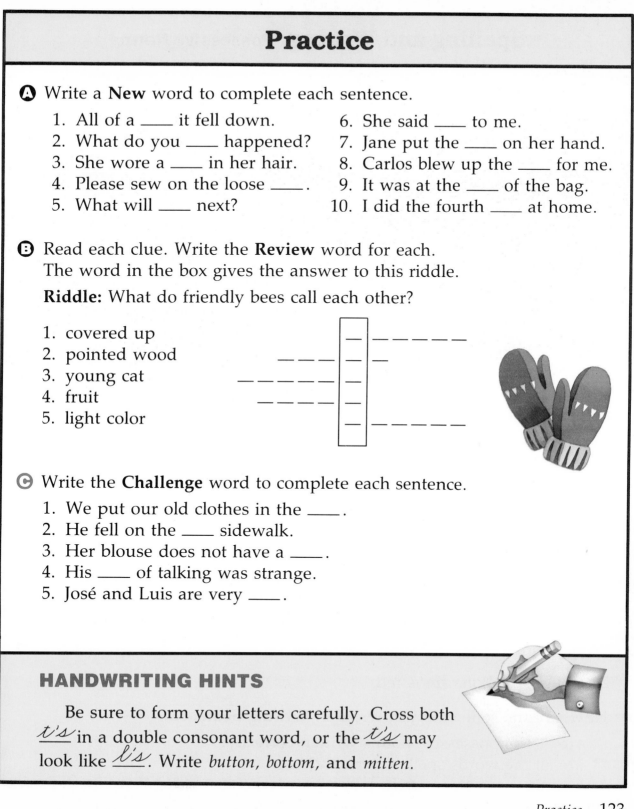

**C** Write the **Challenge** word to complete each sentence.

1. We put our old clothes in the ___.
2. He fell on the ___ sidewalk.
3. Her blouse does not have a ___.
4. His ___ of talking was strange.
5. José and Luis are very ___.

## HANDWRITING HINTS

Be sure to form your letters carefully. Cross both *t's* in a double consonant word, or the *t's* may look like *l's*. Write *button*, *bottom*, and *mitten*.

# Spelling and Writing: Possessive Nouns

A *possessive noun* names who or what has something. Add an *apostrophe* and *s* (**'s**) to the word that does not end with *s*.

    puppets of the <u>teacher</u> = <u>teacher's</u> puppets

Add an *apostrophe* (**'**) to a word that ends with *s*.

    puppets of the <u>teachers</u> = <u>teachers'</u> puppets

## Writing Sentences

Imagine you are watching a puppet show. Write three sentences that tell what happens. Use each possessive noun below in one of your sentences.

1. puppet's ribbon

2. boys' balloon

3. girl's button

## Editing sentences

Look at the special editing symbols. Use them to correct the sentences. Write each sentence correctly.

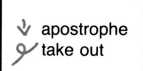

apostrophe
take out

1. The button is for the a cats eye.

2. two girls ribbons are is red.

Now edit the sentences you wrote in **Writing Sentences.**

☐ Are all the possessive nouns written correctly?
☐ Are all the words spelled correctly?

# Review

What letters are missing? Complete each word. Write the word.

**Ⓐ** 1. bu__on
    6. mi__en
    **Ⓑ** 1. ye__ow
    **Ⓒ** 1. a__ic

    2. su__ose
    7. le__on
    2. ki__en
    2. co__ar

    3. ri__on
    8. ba__oon
    3. a__ow
    3. ma__er

    4. he__o
    9. ha__en
    4. a__le
    4. sli__ery

    5. su__en
    10. bo__om
    5. hi__en
    5. di__erent

# Dictionary Skills

When you look up the word *balloon* in your Spelling Dictionary, you find the following:   **bal·loon /bə lün′/**

The first part shows the number of syllables. You can see that *balloon* has two syllables. The second part shows how to say the word. The accent (′) shows which syllable is stressed. In the word *balloon,* the second syllable is stressed.

Look up the word *button* in the Spelling Dictionary. Write the answers to the questions.

1. How many syllables does the word have?
2. Which syllable is stressed?

# Content Words

You may use these double-consonant words in your social studies class.

**tunnel**    **corral**    **cottage**

Write the word to complete each sentence.

1. We live in a ____ in the woods.
2. Jane put the horses in the ____.
3. The ____ went under the river.

## A NEW

jolly
valley
really
turkey
penny
many
alley
happy
merry
party

## B REVIEW

baby
lady
silly
very
funny

## C CHALLENGE

study
easy
probably
hurry
money

/ē/ at the end of a word is spelled **y** as in *strawberry*
**ey** as in *monkey*

Read each word. Look at the ending. Write the words.

1. Which words end with the /ē/ sound spelled **y**?
   Underline the letters that spell the vowel sounds in
   each **New** word.

2. Which words end with the /ē/ sound spelled **ey**?

### HANDWRITING MODELS

• jolly    many    • baby    • study
valley    alley    lady    easy
really    happy    silly    probably
turkey    merry    very    hurry
penny    party    funny    money

# Practice

**Ⓐ** Write a **New** word to complete each sentence.

1. We are going to a birthday ____.
2. Ed has only one ____ to spend.
3. Jorge lives down in the ____.
4. The cat hid in the ____.
5. Is Maria ____ going to the moon?
6. We are ____ with our new house.
7. We ate a ____ for Thanksgiving.
8. The library has ____ books.
9. The man had a ____ smile.
10. It was a very ____ fair.

**Ⓑ** Write the **Review** word to complete each sentence.

Marsha and I are __(1)__ good friends. She has a young __(2)__ brother. A __(3)__ takes care of him. She makes __(4)__ faces. We think she is __(5)__.

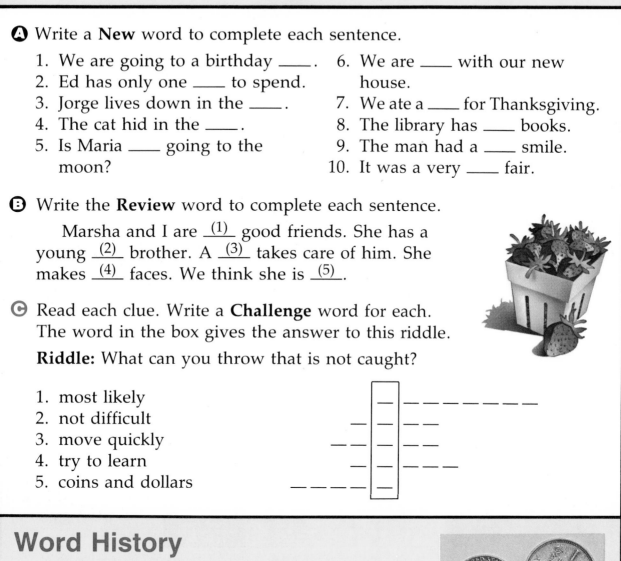

**Ⓒ** Read each clue. Write a **Challenge** word for each. The word in the box gives the answer to this riddle.

**Riddle:** What can you throw that is not caught?

1. most likely
2. not difficult
3. move quickly
4. try to learn
5. coins and dollars

# Word History

The word *penny* comes from the Old English word *pening*. It was the British coin worth a small part of a shilling. The penny is a coin of the United States and is worth one cent.

Choose another word from this Unit and look it up in the dictionary to find out what language it comes from.

# Spelling and Writing: A Friendly Letter

A *friendly letter* is a letter that you write to someone you know well. A friendly letter has many parts.

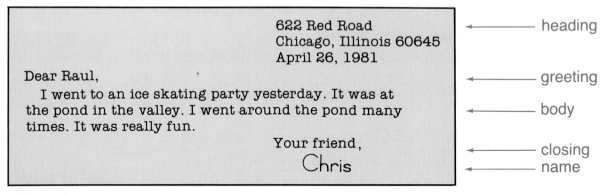

622 Red Road
Chicago, Illinois 60645
April 26, 1981     ←——— heading

Dear Raul,     ←——— greeting
    I went to an ice skating party yesterday. It was at the pond in the valley. I went around the pond many times. It was really fun.     ←——— body

    Your friend,     ←——— closing
    Chris     ←——— name

# Writing a Friendly Letter

The body of a friendly letter is already written below. Write your address and today's date in the heading. Then write your greeting, closing, and name.

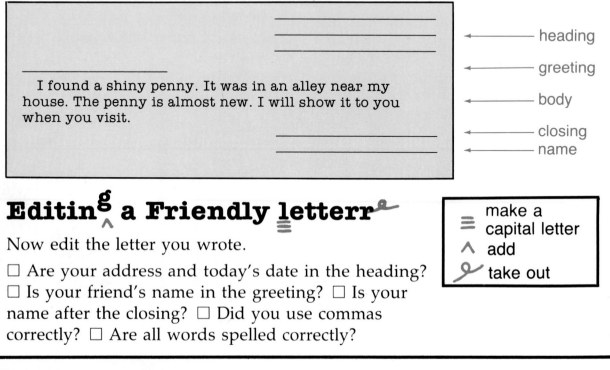

_____     ←——— heading
_____
_____

_____     ←——— greeting

    I found a shiny penny. It was in an alley near my house. The penny is almost new. I will show it to you when you visit.     ←——— body

_____     ←——— closing
_____     ←——— name

# Editing a Friendly letter

Now edit the letter you wrote.

☐ Are your address and today's date in the heading?
☐ Is your friend's name in the greeting? ☐ Is your name after the closing? ☐ Did you use commas correctly? ☐ Are all words spelled correctly?

| | |
|---|---|
| = | make a capital letter |
| ∧ | add |
| ℛ | take out |

# Review

Which ending is correct, *-ey* or *-y?* Complete each
**New, Review,** or **Challenge** word. Write the word.

**Ⓐ** 1. vall__      6. all__
    2. happ__      7. part__
    3. merr__      8. turk__
    4. joll__      9. penn__
    5. man__     10. reall__

**Ⓑ** 1. funn__
    2. sill__
    3. bab__
    4. ver__
    5. lad__

**Ⓒ** 1. hurr__
    2. mon__
    3. eas__
    4. stud__
    5. probabl__

# Word Building

**If a word ends with a consonant and _y_, change the _y_
to _i_ before adding _-es_ or _-ed_.**

    study + es = studies     study + ed = studied

Add the ending to each word. Write the whole word.

1. I found three (penny + es) today.    pennies
2. Ken (try + ed) to catch the bus.
3. We went to two (party + es) this week.
4. The child (hurry + ed) to school.

# Content Words

You may use these /ē/ words in your
science class.

    **poppy**    **donkey**    **body**

Write the word that could join each group.
Use the Spelling Dictionary for help.

1. arm, leg, head, ____
2. rose, tulip, sunflower, ____
3. horse, ox, mule, ____

# THE /ər/ SOUND

/ər/ is spelled **er** as in *tower*
**or** as in *elevator*

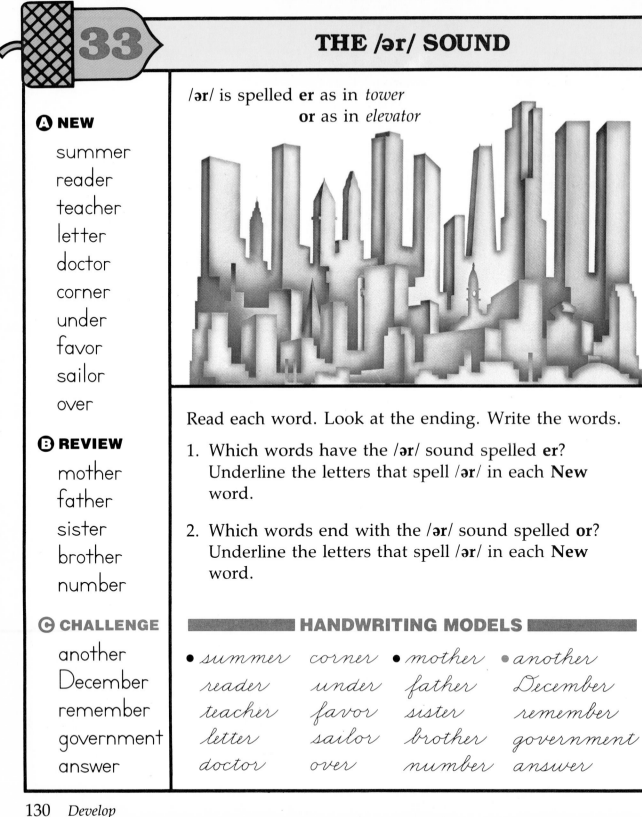

**A NEW**

summer
reader
teacher
letter
doctor
corner
under
favor
sailor
over

**B REVIEW**

mother
father
sister
brother
number

**C CHALLENGE**

another
December
remember
government
answer

Read each word. Look at the ending. Write the words.

1. Which words have the /ər/ sound spelled **er**?
   Underline the letters that spell /ər/ in each **New**
   word.

2. Which words end with the /ər/ sound spelled **or**?
   Underline the letters that spell /ər/ in each **New**
   word.

**HANDWRITING MODELS**

• *summer*    *corner*    • *mother*    • *another*
  *reader*    *under*    *father*    *December*
  *teacher*    *favor*    *sister*    *remember*
  *letter*    *sailor*    *brother*    *government*
  *doctor*    *over*    *number*    *answer*

130   *Develop*

# Practice

**A** Write a **New** word to complete each sentence.

1. His house is around the ___.
2. John is a ___ at our school.
3. My cat sleeps ___ the bed.
4. Please do me a ___.
5. We spent last ___ away.
6. I must write a ___ to Jane.
7. Miss Smith gave us a new ___.
8. My dad was a ___ in the Navy.
9. My friend is coming ___ today.
10. The ___ gave me medicine.

**B** Write the **Review** words to complete the puzzle.

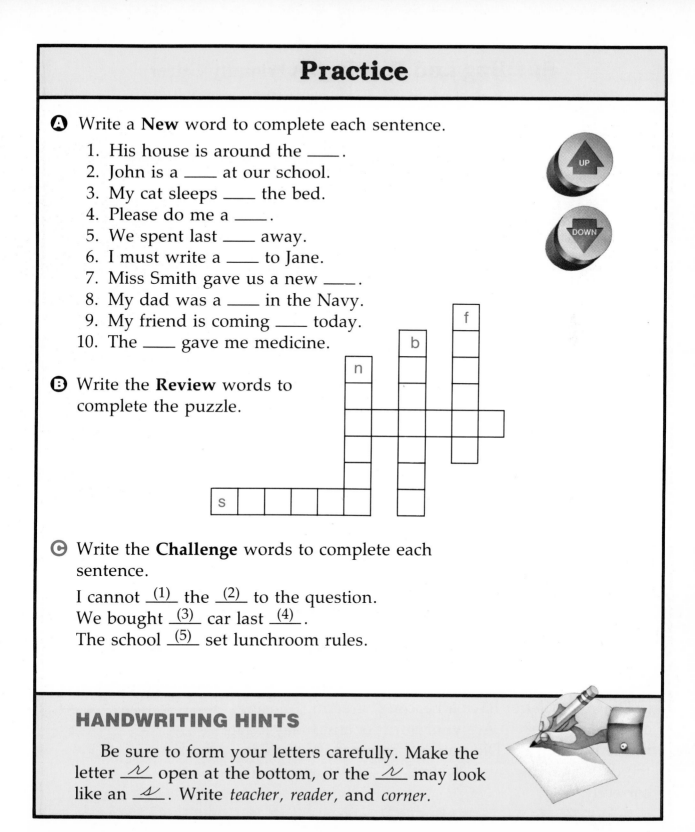

**C** Write the **Challenge** words to complete each sentence.

I cannot __(1)__ the __(2)__ to the question.
We bought __(3)__ car last __(4)__.
The school __(5)__ set lunchroom rules.

## HANDWRITING HINTS

Be sure to form your letters carefully. Make the letter _r_ open at the bottom, or the _r_ may look like an _i_. Write *teacher*, *reader*, and *corner*.

# Spelling and Writing: A Friendly Letter

A *friendly letter* is a letter you write to someone you know well. A friendly letter has many parts.

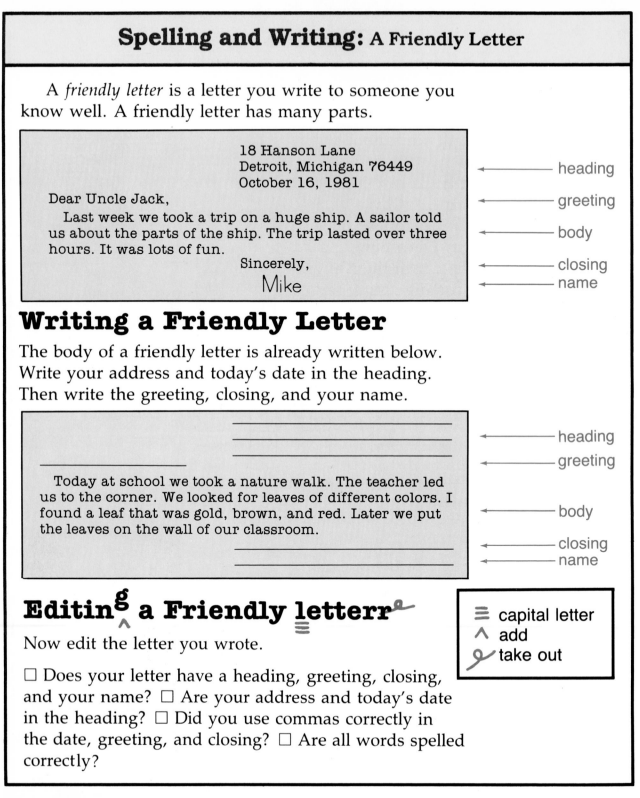

18 Hanson Lane
Detroit, Michigan 76449
October 16, 1981 ←——— heading

Dear Uncle Jack, ←——— greeting

Last week we took a trip on a huge ship. A sailor told us about the parts of the ship. The trip lasted over three hours. It was lots of fun. ←——— body

Sincerely, ←——— closing
Mike ←——— name

## Writing a Friendly Letter

The body of a friendly letter is already written below. Write your address and today's date in the heading. Then write the greeting, closing, and your name.

————— ←——— heading
————— ←——— greeting

Today at school we took a nature walk. The teacher led us to the corner. We looked for leaves of different colors. I found a leaf that was gold, brown, and red. Later we put the leaves on the wall of our classroom. ←——— body

————— ←——— closing
————— ←——— name

## Editing a Friendly letter

Now edit the letter you wrote.

□ Does your letter have a heading, greeting, closing, and your name? □ Are your address and today's date in the heading? □ Did you use commas correctly in the date, greeting, and closing? □ Are all words spelled correctly?

≡ capital letter
∧ add
✄ take out

# Review

What letters are missing? Complete each word. Write
the word.

**A** 1. fav＿＿
2. doct＿＿
3. und＿＿
4. lett＿＿
5. corn＿＿

6. teach＿＿
7. sail＿＿
8. read＿＿
9. ov＿＿
10. summ＿＿

**B** 1. numb＿＿
2. moth＿＿
3. sist＿＿
4. fath＿＿
5. broth＿＿

**C** 1. answ＿＿
2. anoth＿＿
3. rememb＿＿
4. Decemb＿＿
5. gov＿＿nment

# Word Building

Sometimes you can make a new word
by adding _-er_ to the end of a word. The
new word names a person who does a
kind of work.

teach + er = teacher (one who teaches)

Add _-er_ to each word. Write the word.

1. farm + er   farmer
2. climb + er
3. paint + er
4. sing + er

# Content Words

You may use these /ər/ words in your math class.

**lower**      **greater**      **higher**

Write the word to complete each sentence. Use the
Spelling Dictionary for help.

1. A mountain is ＿＿ than a hill.
2. Five is ＿＿ than two.
3. A house is ＿＿ than a skyscraper.

# 34

# WORDS OFTEN CONFUSED

Some words sound the same, but they have different spellings and different meanings.

**A NEW**

its
it's
week
weak
for
four
sent
cent
aunt
ant

**B REVIEW**

one
won
ate
eight
by
buy

**C CHALLENGE**

piece
peace
quite
quiet

Read each word. Think about the spelling and the meaning of each word. Then write the word that matches each clue.

**A**
1. tiny insect
2. mailed
3. given to
4. yours, hers, ___
5. seven days
6. not strong
7. three, ___, five
8. one penny
9. she's, he's, ___
10. uncle and ___

**B**
1. 4 plus 4
2. came in first
3. spend money
4. ___, two, three
5. swallowed
6. near to

**C**
1. calm
2. very
3. silent
4. part of

## ══ HANDWRITING MODELS ══

- *its*    *four*    • *one*    *buy*
  *it's*    *sent*    *won*    • *piece*
  *week*    *cent*    *ate*    *peace*
  *weak*    *aunt*    *eight*    *quite*
  *for*    *ant*    *by*    *quiet*

# Practice

**A** Write the **New** word to complete each sentence.

1. I found an ___ in the sink.
2. I don't have a ___ to spend.
3. There are ___ children here.
4. Mom is very tired and ___ .
5. Now ___ time to leave.
6. My ___ is coming to visit us.
7. We ___ the package last Monday.
8. John bought a gift ___ his mother.
9. Last ___ we went to the circus.
10. What is ___ color?

**B** Write the **Review** word that means nearly the same as the underlined part of each sentence.

1. He will <u>spend money for</u> the book.
2. He <u>swallowed</u> the fruit.
3. He had only <u>a</u> minute.
4. There were <u>two more than six</u>.
5. They came <u>near</u> the house.
6. My team <u>came in first</u>.

**C** Write the **Challenge** word that means the same as the underlined word or words in each sentence.

1. She was <u>not talking</u>.
2. That is <u>very</u> heavy.
3. May I have a <u>part</u> of the pie?
4. There was <u>order</u> between the two.

## HANDWRITING HINTS

Be sure to form your letters carefully. If an _ℳ_ does not touch the line, the _ℳ_ may look like an _ℳ_ . Write *cent*, *ant*, and *one*.

# Spelling and Writing: An Envelope

An *envelope* is used to send a friendly letter. An envelope includes the name and address of the person receiving the letter, the name and address of the person writing the letter, and a stamp. The ZIP code follows the name of the state.

Read the following envelope.

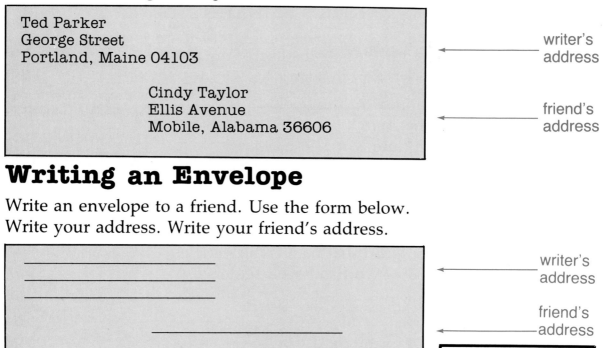

Ted Parker
George Street
Portland, Maine 04103
— writer's address

Cindy Taylor
Ellis Avenue
Mobile, Alabama 36606
— friend's address

# Writing an Envelope

Write an envelope to a friend. Use the form below. Write your address. Write your friend's address.

— writer's address

— friend's address

≡ capital letter
∧ add
℘ take out

# Editing an envelope

Now edit the envelope you wrote in **Writing An Envelope.**

☐ Do all names of people and places begin with capital letters? ☐ Does a comma come between the name of the city and the state? ☐ Are all the words spelled correctly?

# Review

Write the words to complete each sentence.

**A** He has been w _(1)_ for a w _(2)_ .  **B** He a _(1)_ his dinner at e _(2)_ .

Pam sleeps f _(3)_ nearly f _(4)_ hours.

We b _(3)_ our milk b _(4)_ the quart.

Jan s _(5)_ me a fifty c _(6)_ check.

Our team w _(5)_ by o _(6)_ point.

My a _(7)_ is afraid of an a _(8)_ .

**C** We gave each a p _(1)_ to keep p _(2)_ .

I think i _(9)_ losing i _(10)_ color.

Try not to be q _(3)_ so q _(4)_ .

# Word Building

The letters _-ent_ are a spelling pattern. If you can spell _sent_, you may figure out how to spell _tent_.

Add _-ent_ to the letters below. Write the new words.

**-ent**   1. b _____   bent
2. sp _____
3. w _____
4. r _____

# Content Words

You may use these words in your reading class.

**days    daze    sail    sale**

Write the words to complete each sentence. Use the Spelling Dictionary for help.

He bought a new _(1)_ for the boat at the _(2)_ .
He was in a _(3)_ for many _(4)_ .

# 35

# THEME: ANIMALS

## A NEW

seal
tiger
giraffe
squirrel
camel
whale
rabbit
skunk
shark
buffalo

## B REVIEW

lion
bear
horse
fox
sheep

## C CHALLENGE

dinosaur
octopus
kangaroo
chimpanzee
pigeon

Have you been to the zoo lately? Were you able to name all the animals? The words in this lesson can help you. They name different kinds of animals.

Read each word. Write the name that matches each clue.

**A**
1. lived on the plains
2. can do water tricks
3. has a long neck
4. has humps
5. can smell bad
6. has stripes
7. huge sea animal
8. stores up nuts
9. likes carrots
10. has a sharp fin

**B**
1. runs in races
2. sly animal
3. the jungle king
4. has a coat of wool
5. likes honey

**C**
1. kind of ape
2. hops a lot
3. lived long ago
4. flies in the city
5. has eight arms

## HANDWRITING MODELS

- seal
tiger
giraffe
squirrel
camel

whale
rabbit
skunk
shark
buffalo

- lion
bear
horse
fox
sheep

- dinosaur
octopus
kangaroo
chimpanzee
pigeon

# Practice

**A** Find the ten animals in the puzzle. The words go →, ↓, or ↘. Then write each word.

```
s e a l m n o p w
k q b s h a r k h
u b u f f a l o a
n l f i j k l m l
k e g i r a f f e
s t i g e r p i a
t i p c a m e l p
r a b b i t o l t
```

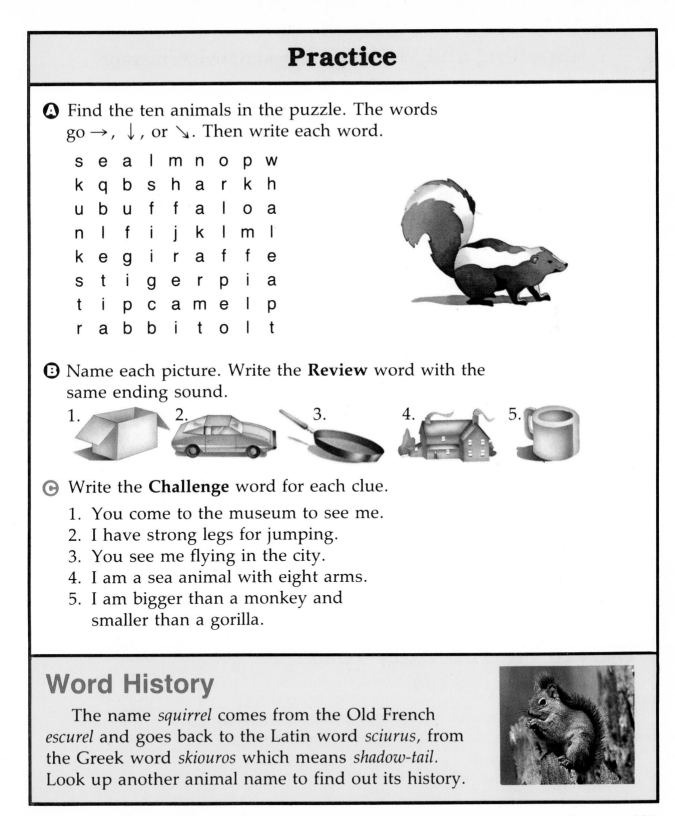

**B** Name each picture. Write the **Review** word with the same ending sound.

1. 2. 3. 4. 5.

**C** Write the **Challenge** word for each clue.

1. You come to the museum to see me.
2. I have strong legs for jumping.
3. You see me flying in the city.
4. I am a sea animal with eight arms.
5. I am bigger than a monkey and smaller than a gorilla.

## Word History

The name *squirrel* comes from the Old French *escurel* and goes back to the Latin word *sciurus*, from the Greek word *skiouros* which means *shadow-tail*. Look up another animal name to find out its history.

# Spelling and Writing: A Descriptive Paragraph

A *friendly letter* has a *heading, greeting, body, closing,* and *name.* The body can be a *descriptive paragraph.* The paragraph tells how something looks, sounds, feels, tastes, or smells. Read the friendly letter on the right.

7 Down Lane
Warren, Ohio 44322
March 8, 1981

Dear Bob,
   I saw a funny seal at the zoo. The brown seal keeps a ball on its nose. It splashes water with its flippers. The seal makes funny noises.

      Sincerely,
      Kim

# Writing a Friendly Letter

Write a friendly letter to someone you know. In the body, write a descriptive paragraph that tells about a giraffe at the zoo. Start the paragraph with this main idea sentence: *The zoo has an interesting giraffe.* Then write three detail sentences that tell more about the giraffe.

# Editing a Friendly letter

Now edit the letter you wrote.

☐ Does your letter have a heading, greeting, closing, and your name? ☐ Did you indent the first word in the body? ☐ Did you use commas correctly? ☐ Are all words spelled correctly?

| | |
|---|---|
| = | make a capital letter |
| ∧ | add |
| ℓ | take out |

# Review

What letters are missing? Complete each word.
Write the word.

**Ⓐ**
1. bu__alo
2. __unk
3. __ale
4. squi__el
5. tig__
6. s__l
7. gira__e
8. c_m_l
9. ra__it
10. __ark

**Ⓑ**
1. h__se
2. sh__p
3. l__n
4. b__r
5. f_x

**Ⓒ**
1. pi___n
2. kangar__
3. dinos__r
4. oct_p_s
5. ch_mp_nz__

# Dictionary Skills

Words in a dictionary are in ABC order.

**wh__a__t      wh__e__n      wh__y__**

When a set of words begins with the *same* two letters, use the **third** letter to put the words in ABC order.

Write each set of words in ABC order.

1. **bee**
   **bed**
   **bear**

2. **lion**
   **lid**
   **lip**

# Content Words

You may use these animal words in your reading class.

**chipmunk      porcupine      rooster**

Write the words to complete each sentence. Use the Spelling Dictionary for help.

A __(1)__ is a member of the bird family.
Two rodents are the __(2)__ and the __(3)__.

# UNIT 36   REVIEW: UNITS 31-35

## UNIT 31

Many words have double consonants in the middle.
The double consonant has only one sound.

balloon      hello        happen       button      bottom
ribbon       suppose      mitten       sudden      lesson

Read each clue. Write the words to complete the puzzle.

**Across**
3. the opposite of top
5. to fasten
7. to come to pass
8. to imagine
9. rubber bag filled with air

**Down**
1. something to be learned
2. a band worn in the hair
4. a covering for the hand
6. without being warned
7. a greeting

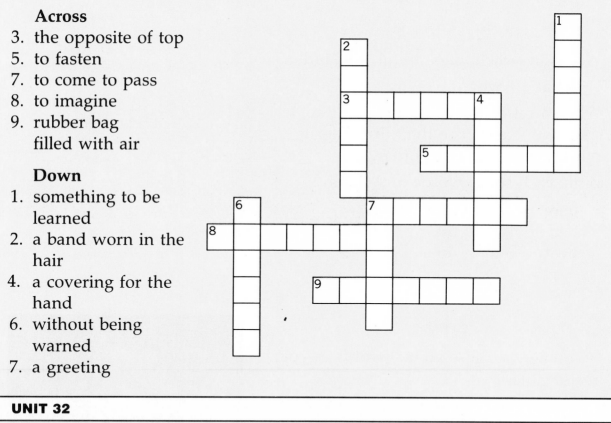

## UNIT 32

/ē/ at the end of a word is spelled **y** or **ey**

jolly        valley       really       turkey      penny
many         alley        happy        party       merry

Write the /ē/ words in ABC order.

142   *Review: Units 31–35*

## UNIT 33

/ər/ is spelled **er** or **or**

| summer | reader | teacher | letter | doctor |
|--------|--------|---------|--------|--------|
| corner | under | favor | sailor | over |

Write the word that belongs in each group.

1. goodness, kindness, ____
2. hospital, nurse, ____
3. beneath, below, ____
4. card, note, ____
5. edges meet, streets meet, ____
6. classroom, children, ____
7. ocean, ship, ____
8. book, story, ____
9. above, on top of, ____
10. winter, spring, ____

## UNIT 34

Some words sound the same, but have different spellings and different meanings.

| its | week | for | sent | aunt |
|-----|------|-----|------|------|
| it's | weak | four | cent | ant |

Write the correct word for each meaning.

1. tiny insect
2. your mother's or father's sister
3. having very little power
4. seven days
5. 2 + 2
6. because of
7. whose
8. it is
9. one penny
10. mailed

Some words are the names of animals.

| | | | | |
|---|---|---|---|---|
| seal | tiger | whale | rabbit | giraffe |
| squirrel | skunk | shark | camel | buffalo |

Name each picture. Write the name for each animal.

1.

2.

3.

4.

5.

6

7.

8.

9.

10.

# Word Building

Add the beginning or ending to each word. Write the whole word.

1. The zoo now has four (giraffe + s).    giraffes
2. Please help Tom (un + button) his coat.
3. We read about an (under + water) trip.
4. The (turkey + s) made a lot of noise.
5. We have had nice (summer + y) weather.
6. The dog ran into the (alley + way).
7. A dime is worth ten (penny + es).
8. Now you must (re + button) your coat.
9. I am (suppose + ed) to go home now.
10. We are (suppose + ing) that it will rain.

Mark the word in each group that is not
spelled correctly.

1. a. its      b. bottom        2. a. squirrel    b. button        1. ⓐⓑⓒ⬤
   c. ribbon   d. bloon            c. ribbon      d. merry         2. ⓐⓑⓒⓓ

3. a. under    b. mitten        4. a. really      b. reader        3. ⓐⓑⓒⓓ
   c. kitten   d. reder            c. penny       d. camal         4. ⓐⓑⓒⓓ

5. a. realy    b. corner        6. a. fox         b. apple         5. ⓐⓑⓒⓓ
   c. teacher  d. favor            c. mother      d. hapen         6. ⓐⓑⓒⓓ

7. a. seel     b. father        8. a. sailor      b. balloon       7. ⓐⓑⓒⓓ
   c. letter   d. one              c. meny        d. happen        8. ⓐⓑⓒⓓ

9. a. under    b. funny        10. a. over        b. it's          9. ⓐⓑⓒⓓ
   c. baby     d. hellow           c. botton      d. ate          10. ⓐⓑⓒⓓ

11. a. bear    b. yellow       12. a. hello       b. wek          11. ⓐⓑⓒⓓ
    c. party   d. docter           c. summer      d. sister       12. ⓐⓑⓒⓓ

13. a. button  b. ribben       14. a. weak        b. techer       13. ⓐⓑⓒⓓ
    c. four    d. happen           c. for         d. suppose      14. ⓐⓑⓒⓓ

15. a. supose  b. father       16. a. leter       b. mitten       15. ⓐⓑⓒⓓ
    c. merry   d. sudden           c. corner      d. party        16. ⓐⓑⓒⓓ

17. a. really  b. penney       18. a. turkey      b. joly         17. ⓐⓑⓒⓓ
    c. jolly   d. skunk            c. sailor      d. valley       18. ⓐⓑⓒⓓ

19. a. aunt    b. sumer        20. a. four        b. shark        19. ⓐⓑⓒⓓ
    c. many    d. sent             c. parte       d. for          20. ⓐⓑⓒⓓ

21. a. turky   b. ant          22. a. faver       b. rabbit       21. ⓐⓑⓒⓓ
    c. lesson  d. number           c. whale       d. giraffe      22. ⓐⓑⓒⓓ

23. a. jolly   b. vally        24. a. undr        b. brother      23. ⓐⓑⓒⓓ
    c. cent    d. lesson           c. alley       d. squirrel     24. ⓐⓑⓒⓓ

# GUIDE TO PRONUNCIATION

| | | | |
|---|---|---|---|
| /a/ | hat | /ch/ | chin |
| /ā/ | ape | /d/ | dot |
| /ä/ | father | /f/ | five |
| /är/ | car | /g/ | game |
| /ãr/ | dare | /h/ | hot |
| /e/ | pet | /hw/ | wheel |
| /ē/ | me | /j/ | joke |
| /ėr/ | term | /k/ | kit |
| /i/ | pig | /l/ | lid |
| /ī/ | ice | /m/ | man |
| /ir/ | dear | /n/ | nest |
| /o/ | hot | /ng/ | long |
| /ō/ | old | /p/ | pail |
| /ô/ | dog | /r/ | ride |
| /oi/ | oil | /s/ | sock |
| /ôr/ | fork | /sh/ | shoe |
| /ou/ | out | /t/ | tag |
| /u/ | mud | /th/ | thin |
| /ů/ | put | /<u>th</u>/ | mother |
| /ü/ | tool | /v/ | vest |
| /ū/ | cute | /w/ | wet |
| /ə/ | ago | /y/ | yarn |
| /ər/ | letter | /z/ | zoo |
| /b/ | bat | /zh/ | division |

# SPELLING DICTIONARY

## A

**about**   1. That book is *about* John F. Kennedy. 2. There were *about* twenty people waiting for the bus.
  **a·bout** /ə bout´/ *preposition; adverb.*

**across**   1. We came *across* in a rowboat. 2. The cat walked *across* our path.
  **a·cross** /ə krôs´/ *adverb; preposition.*

**add**   To find the sum of two or more numbers. If you *add* 2 and 7, you get 9.
  **add** /ad/ *verb,* **added, adding.**

**adjective**   A word that tells something about a noun or a pronoun. An adjective describes a person, place, or thing.
  **ad·jec·tive** /aj´ik tiv/ *noun, plural* **adjectives.**

**adventure**   An exciting or unusual experience. Their first trip by airplane was an *adventure* for the boys.
  **ad·ven·ture** /ad ven´chər/ *noun, plural* **adventures.**

**after**   1. It is ten minutes *after* three o'clock. 2. I came on Sunday and he came one day *after*. 3. It happened *after* you left.
  **af·ter** /af´tər/ *preposition; adverb; conjunction.*

**afternoon**   The part of the day between noon and evening.

**af·ter·noon** /af´tər nün/ *noun, plural* **afternoons.**

**again**   Once more; another time. She did not hear him the first time, so he called to her *again*.
  **a·gain** /ə gen´/ *adverb.*

**all**   1. The whole of. We ate *all* the ice cream. 2. Every one. Students from *all* the schools in town were in the swimming meet. 3. Everything or everyone. *All* were saved from the fire. 4. The whole amount or number. *All* of us are going to the party. 5. Completely. The work is *all* finished.
  **all** /ôl/ *adjective; noun; pronoun; adverb.*

**alley**   A narrow street between buildings. There is an *alley* behind those apartments.
  **al·ley** /al´ē/ *noun, plural* **alleys.**

**am**   I *am* happy that you can come to my birthday party.
  **am** /am/ *or* /əm/ *verb.*

**amount**   What something adds up to. What is the *amount* of money you spent?
  **a·mount** /ə mount´/ *noun, plural* **amounts.**

**an**   He ate *an* apple. We saw *an* elephant.
  **an** /an/ *or* /ən/ *indefinite article.*

**and**  It is tall *and* strong. Susan *and* Jane came to visit me. I can run *and* hop.
  **and** /and/ *or* /ənd/ *conjunction*.

**ankle**  The joint that connects the foot and the leg.
  **an·kle** /ang′kəl/ *noun, plural* **ankles**.

**another**  I want *another* piece of cake.
  **an·oth·er** /ə nu<u>th</u>′ər/ *adjective*.

**answer**  **1.** Something written, said, or done in reply. **2.** Solution to a problem.
  **an·swer** /an′sər/ *noun, plural* **answers**.

**ant**  A small insect like bees or wasps.
  **ant** /ant/ *noun, plural* **ants**.

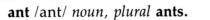

ant

**any**  **1.** Take *any* seat. **2.** He runs faster than *any* of the other boys. **3.** Stop before you go *any* farther.
  **an·y** /en′ē/ *adjective; pronoun; adverb*.

**anything**  I'll do *anything* you ask me to.
  **an·y·thing** /en′ē thing′/ *pronoun*.

**anyway**  It's raining, but we are going for a walk *anyway*.
  **an·y·way** /en′ē wā′/ *adverb*.

**apostrophe**  A punctuation mark (′) used in the following ways: **1.** To show that a letter or letters have been left out in a word or words. For example, "you're" means "you are." The apostrophe has taken the place of the *a* in *are*. **2.** To show that something belongs to a person or thing. "Paul's dog" means "the dog that belongs to Paul."
  **a·pos·tro·phe** /ə pos′trə fē/ *noun, plural* **apostrophes**.

**apple**  A fruit with red, yellow, or green skin that grows on trees.
  **ap·ple** /ap′əl/ *noun, plural* **apples**.

**April**  The fourth month of the year.
  **A·pril** /ā′prəl/ *noun*.

**aren't**  Why *aren't* you going?
  **aren't** /ärnt/ *contraction* for **are not**.

**arm**  The part of the body between the shoulder and the wrist.
  **arm** /ärm/ *noun, plural* **arms**.

**arrow**  A slender stick that has a sharp point at one end and feathers at the other, made to be shot from a bow.
  **ar·row** /ar′ō/ *noun, plural* **arrows**.

**art**  Painting, drawing, and sculpture.
  **art** /ärt/ *noun, plural* **arts**.

**as**  **1.** The second movie was not *as* good *as* the first. **2.** Bob arrived *as* we left. **3.** I'm speaking *as* your friend.
  **as** /az/ *adverb; conjunction; preposition*.

**at**  **1.** The race starts *at* the top of the hill. **2.** He looked *at* the picture.
  **at** /at/ *preposition*.

**ate**  We *ate* all the pie.
  **ate** /āt/ *verb*.

**attic**  The storage space or room just below the roof of the house.
  **at·tic** /at′ik/ *noun, plural* **attics**.

**aunt**  **1.** The sister of one's mother or father. **2.** The wife of one's uncle.
  **aunt** /ant/ *or* /änt/ *noun, plural* **aunts**.

**awful**  **1.** Terrible. **2.** Very bad.
  **aw·ful** /ô′fəl/ *adjective*.

**B**

**baby**  A very young child; infant.
  **ba·by** /bā′bē/ *noun, plural* **babies**.

**bad**  Not good. That was a *bad* program.
  **bad** /bad/ *adjective*, **worse, worst**.

**ball** 1. A round object. Bill wound the kite string into a *ball*. 2. A roundish object used in various games. John brought his *ball* and bat for the baseball game.
　**ball** /bôl/ *noun, plural* **balls.**

**balloon** A bag filled with air or gas.
　**bal·loon** /bə lün′/ *noun, plural* **balloons.**

**bead** A small round piece of glass, wood, plastic, or other material. A bead has a hole through it so that it can be strung on a wire or string.
　**bead** /bēd/ *noun, plural* **beads.**

**bear** A large animal with shaggy fur.
　**bear** /bãr/ *noun, plural* **bears.**

**became** My sister *became* a lawyer.
　**be·came** /bi kām′/ *verb.*

**because** For the reason that. Phil is cold *because* he did not wear his sweater.
　**be·cause** /bi kôz′/ *conjunction.*

**been** I have *been* sick with a cold.
　**been** /bin/ *verb.*

**before** In front of; ahead of. Ed stood *before* me in line. A comes *before* B.
　**be·fore** /bi fôr′/ *preposition.*

**believe** To have trust or faith in the truth of. Jack *believes* in ghosts.
　**be·lieve** /bi lēv′/ *verb,* **believed, believing.**

**belt** A strip or band of cloth, leather, or other material worn around the waist.
　**belt** /belt/ *noun, plural* **belts.**

**bent** 1. He *bent* the hanger in half. 2. He found a *bent* nail on the floor.
　**bent** /bent/ *verb; adjective.*

**bird** An animal that has wings and a body covered with feathers.
　**bird** /bėrd/ *noun, plural* **birds.**

**birth** The beginning of life of a person or animal. We saw the *birth* of a chick.
　**birth** /bėrth/ *noun, plural* **births.**

**birthday** The day on which a person is born. My *birthday* is on May 12.
　**birth·day** /bėrth′dā/ *noun, plural* **birthdays.**

**blind** 1. Unable to see. The boy helped the *blind* man across the street. 2. To make unable to see. The sun will *blind* you if you look at it too long.
　**blind** /blīnd/ *adjective,* **blinder, blindest;** *verb,* **blinded, blinding.**

**blossom** The flower of a plant or tree that produces fruit.
　**blos·som** /blos′əm/ *noun, plural* **blossoms.**

blossom

**blow** 1. Hard hit or stroke made with the fist, a weapon, or some object. 2. To move with speed or force. A breeze *blew* the leaves across the yard. 3. To send out a strong current of air. *Blow* on your hands to warm them.
　**blow** /blō/ *noun, plural* **blows;** *verb,* **blew, blown, blowing.**

at; āges; fäther; cär; dãring; end; mē; tėrm; it; tīger; souvenir; hot; ōld; ôff; oil; fôrk; out; up; fůll; trüly; mūsic; sing; thin; zh in treasure; ə in lemon, ago, pencil, taken, circus; ər in letter, honor, dollar.

**board** **1.** A long, flat piece of sawed wood. **2.** To get on a ship, plane, or train. We will *board* a ship for England.
**board** /bôrd/ *noun, plural* **boards;** *verb,* **boarded, boarding.**

**boat** A small vessel that is used for traveling on water.
**boat** /bōt/ *noun, plural* **boats.**

boat

**body** All of a person, animal, or plant.
**bod·y** /bod′ē/ *noun, plural* **bodies.**

**boil** **1.** To form bubbles and give off steam. Water will *boil* if you heat it enough **2.** To cook by boiling.
**boil** /boil/ *verb,* **boiled, boiling.**

**book** Sheets of paper fastened together between two covers. The pages of a ′book have writing or printing on them.
**book** /bůk/ *noun, plural* **books.**

**border** **1.** A boundary line. They crossed the *border* between the states. **2.** A strip along the edge of anything. Sue's skirt has a pretty red *border.*
**bor·der** /bôr′dər/ *noun, plural* **borders.**

**born** Brought into life or being.
**born** /bôrn/ *adjective.*

**bottom** **1.** The lowest part. **2.** The under part. The *bottom* of the boat is red.
**bot·tom** /bot′əm/ *noun, plural* **bottoms.**

**bought** We *bought* groceries at the store.
**bought** /bôt/ *verb.*

**box** A container used to hold things.

A box is made of cardboard, wood, or another heavy material. It has four sides, a bottom, and sometimes a top.
**box** /boks/ *noun, plural* **boxes.**

**boy** A male child from birth to the time he is a young man.
**boy** /boi/ *noun, plural* **boys.**

**brake** **1.** Something used to stop or slow the movement of a vehicle. **2.** To cause something to stop or slow down by using a brake.
**brake** /brāk/ *noun, plural* **brakes;** *verb,* **braked, braking.**

**brave** Having courage; facing danger or pain without being afraid.
**brave** /brāv/ *adjective,* **braver, bravest.**

**break** **1.** To make come to pieces by force. **2.** To harm or damage. **3.** To fail to obey. Driving too fast *breaks* the law.
**break** /brāk/ *verb,* **broke, broken, breaking.**

**breakfast** The first meal of the day.
**break·fast** /brek′fəst/ *noun, plural* **breakfasts.**

**bright** **1.** Giving much light. The *bright* light hurt her eyes. **2.** Clear; strong. The chair is *bright* red. **3.** Smart, clever. Sarah is a *bright* student.
**bright** /brīt/ *adjective,* **brighter, brightest.**

**bring** **1.** To cause something or someone to come with you. Remember to *bring* your books home. **2.** To cause something to come or happen. The heavy rains will *bring* floods.
**bring** /bring/ *verb,* **brought, bringing.**

**broom** **1.** A brush with a long handle used for sweeping. **2.** A bush with long branches and yellow flowers.

**broom** /brüm/ or /bùm/ *noun, plural* **brooms.**

**brother** A boy or man having the same parents as another person.
**broth·er** /bru<u>th</u>′ər/ *noun, plural* **brothers.**

**brought** Ted *brought* me a present.
**brought** /brôt/ *verb.*

**brown** **1.** A dark color like chocolate or coffee. **2.** Having the color brown.
**brown** /broun/ *noun, plural* **browns;** *adjective,* **browner, brownest.**

**buffalo** A North American wild ox. A *buffalo* has a big shaggy head with short horns and a humped back.
**buf·fa·lo** /buf′ə lō/ *noun, plural* **buffaloes** or **buffalos** or **buffalo.**

**bug** Any of a group of insects.
**bug** /bug/ *noun, plural* **bugs.**

**built** The boys *built* a tree hut.
**built** /bilt/ *verb.*

**bull** The full-grown male of cattle.
**bull** /bùl/ *noun, plural* **bulls.**

**but** Tom is tall, *but* his sister is short.
**but** /but/ *conjunction.*

**button** **1.** Something used to fasten clothing. **2.** A knob that is turned or pushed to make something work.
**but·ton** /but′ən/ *noun, plural* **buttons.**

**buy** To pay money for something.
**buy** /bī/ *verb,* **bought, buying.**

**by** **1.** There is a table *by* the bed. **2.** That book was written *by* E. B. White. **3.** My friend's house is close *by.*
**by** /bī/ *preposition; adverb.*

## C

**calendar** A chart showing the days, weeks, and months of a year.

**cal·en·dar** /kal′ən dər/ *noun, plural* **calendars.**

**calf** **1.** A young cow or bull. **2.** The fleshy part of the back of the leg, between the knee and the ankle.
**calf** /kaf/ *noun, plural* **calves.**

**call** **1.** To speak or say in a loud voice. **2.** To telephone.
**call** /kôl/ *verb,* **called, calling.**

**camel** A large animal with a humped back, long legs, and a long neck.
**cam·el** /kam′əl/ *noun, plural* **camels.**

camel

**camera** A device for taking photographs or motion pictures.
**cam·er·a** /kam′ər ə/ *or* /kam′rə/ *noun, plural* **cameras.**

**can** **1.** She *can* walk faster than you. **2.** *Can* you fix the broken radio? **3.** A container made of metal. Please put the old rags in the garbage *can.*
**can** /kan/ *verb; noun, plural* **cans.**

**cannot** I *cannot* come tomorrow.
**can·not** /kan′ot/ *or* /ka not′/ *verb.*

at; āges; fä<u>th</u>er; cär; dåring; end; mē; tėrm; it; tīger; souven**ir**; hot; ōld; ôff; oil; fôrk; out; up; fùll; trüly; mūsic; sing; <u>th</u>in; **zh** in treasure; ə in lemon, ago, pencil, taken, circus; ər in letter, honor, dollar.

**can't** I *can't* go; I have to study.
can't /kant/ contraction for **cannot.**

**capital** A large form of a letter of the alphabet. *A, B, C,* and *D* are *capitals.*
cap·i·tal /kap'it əl/ *noun, plural* **capitals;** *adjective.*

**captain** **1.** A person who is the leader of a group. Susan was *captain* of the team **2.** A person in charge of a ship. My uncle is the *captain* of a fishing boat.
cap·tain /kap'tən/ *noun, plural* **captains.**

**car** An automobile. A car is a vehicle with four wheels and an engine.
car /kär/ *noun, plural* **cars.**

**case** A box or other container made to hold or cover something.
case /kās/ *noun, plural* **cases.**

**cent** A coin of the United States and Canada. One penny.
cent /sent/ *noun, plural* **cents.**

**center** The middle point, part, or place of anything.
cen·ter /sen'tər/ *noun, plural* **centers.**

**chart** A sheet of information arranged 'in lists, diagrams, tables, and graphs.
chart /chärt/ *noun, plural* **charts.**

**check** **1.** A mark (✔) used to show that something has been approved or is correct. **2.** A written order directing a bank to pay a certain amount of money.
check /chek/ *noun, plural* **checks.**

**cherry** A small, round red fruit with a smooth skin and a central hard pit.
cher·ry /cher'ē/ *noun, plural* **cherries.**

**child** A young boy or girl.
child /chīld/ *noun, plural* **children.**

**chimpanzee** A small African ape that has brownish-black hair.
chim·pan·zee /chim'pan zē'/ *or* /chim pan'zē/ *noun, plural* **chimpanzees.**

**chipmunk** A very small animal with brown fur and dark striped back and tail. Chipmunks belong to the rodent family.
chip·munk /chip'mungk'/ *noun, plural* **chipmunks.**

chipmunk

**circus** A show with trained animals and acrobats, clowns, and other people who do special things.
cir·cus /sèr'kəs/ *noun, plural* **circuses.**

**city** A large area where many people live and work.
cit·y /sit'ē/ *noun, plural* **cities.**

**classroom** A room for classes.
class·room /klas'rüm'/ *or* /klas'rum'/ *noun, plural* **classrooms.**

**claw** A sharp, curved nail on the foot of a bird or animal.
claw /klô/ *noun, plural* **claws.**

**clay** A kind of fine earth. Clay is used to make pottery and bricks.
clay /klā/ *noun, plural* **clays.**

**climb** **1.** To move or go upward. **2.** The act of climbing.
climb /klīm/ *verb,* **climbed, climbing;** *noun, plural* **climbs.**

**clothes** Things worn to cover the body. Betty hung her coat, dresses, skirts, and other *clothes* neatly in the closet.
clothes /klōz/ *or* /klōthz/ *noun plural.*

**clown** A circus person who makes people laugh by doing tricks or stunts.

**clown** /kloun/ *noun, plural* **clowns.**

**clue** A hint that helps solve a problem or mystery. If you can't solve the riddle, I'll give you a *clue.*

**clue** /klü/ *noun, plural* **clues.**

**coast** **1.** The land next to the sea; seashore. **2.** To ride or slide along without effort or power. We *coasted* down the hill on our sleds.

**coast** /kōst/ *noun, plural* **coasts;** *verb,* **coasted, coasting.**

**collar** A band or strap that is worn around the neck. Our dog has a *collar.*

**col·lar** /kol'ər/ *noun, plural* **collars.**

**colt** A young horse.

**colt** /kōlt/ *noun, plural* **colts.**

**comb** **1.** A piece of plastic, metal, or other material that has teeth used to smooth, arrange, or fasten the hair, or to straighten out fibers of wool or cotton before spinning. **2.** To smooth or arrange with a comb.

**comb** /kōm/ *noun, plural* **combs;** *verb,* **combed, combing.**

**come** **1.** To move toward. Please *come* here a minute. **2.** To reach a place; arrive.

**come** /kum/ *verb,* **came, come, coming.**

**comma** A mark of punctuation (,) used to separate ideas or things in a series.

**com·ma** /kom'ə/ *noun, plural* **commas.**

**consonant** A letter of the alphabet that is not a vowel, like *b, f, g, m, p,* and *t.*

**con·so·nant** /kon'sə nənt/ *noun, plural* **consonants.**

**contraction** A short form of two or more words. *Isn't* is the contraction for *is not. He's* is the contraction for *he is.*

**con·trac·tion** /kən trak'shən/ *noun, plural* **contractions.**

**corner** The place or point where two lines or surfaces come together.

**cor·ner** /kôr'nər/ *noun, plural* **corners.**

**corral** A space with a fence around it used for cattle, horses, and other animals.

**cor·ral** /kə ral'/ *noun, plural* **corrals.**

**cost** **1.** Price. The *cost* of that book is five dollars. **2.** To be gotten or bought at the price of. The bicycle *cost* too much, so my father didn't buy it.

**cost** /kôst/ *noun, plural* **costs;** *verb,* **cost, costing.**

**cottage** A small house.

**cot·tage** /kot'ij/ *noun, plural* **cottages.**

cottage

**cough** To force air from the lungs with a sudden, sharp sound.

**cough** /kôf/ *verb,* **coughed, coughing.**

**could** I *could* tell that he was angry.

**could** /kùd/ *verb.*

**couldn't** The little boy *couldn't* reach the high shelf.

**could·n't** /kùd'ənt/ *contraction* for **could not.**

at; āges; fäther; cär; dãring; end; mē; tèrm; it; tīger; souvenir; hot; ōld; ôff; oil; fôrk; out; up; fùll; trüly; mūsic; sing; thin; zh in treasure; ə in lemon, ago, pencil, taken, circus; ər in letter, honor, dollar.

**count** 1. To find out how many of something there are; add up. 2. To say or write down numbers in order.
  count /kount/ *verb*, **counted, counting.**
**course** 1. A way; route; track. 2. An area used for certain sports or games. 3. A series of classes or lessons.
  course /kôrs/ *noun, plural* **courses.**
**cousin** The child of an aunt or uncle.
  cou·sin /kuz′in/ *noun, plural* **cousins.**
**crawl** 1. To move very slowly. Babies *crawl* on their hands and knees. 2. A very slow movement. 3. A fast swimming stroke.
  crawl /krôl/ *verb*, **crawled, crawling;** *noun, plural* **crawls.**
**cube** A solid figure with six equal, square sides.
  cube /cūb/ *noun, plural* **cubes.**

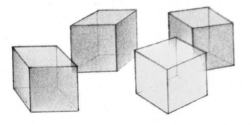

cubes

**cupcake** A small cake.
  cup·cake /kup′kāk′/ *noun, plural* **cup-cakes.**
**cure** To make a sick person or animal healthy again.
  cure /cūr/ *verb*, **cured, curing.**
**curl** 1. To twist in curved rings or coils. She *curled* her hair for the party. 2. A curved lock of hair; ringlet.
  curl /kurl/ *verb*, **curled, curling;** *noun, plural* **curls.**

**curtain** A piece of cloth hung across an open space at windows, in doorways, and across the front part of a stage.
  cur·tain /kèr′tin/ *noun, plural* **curtains.**
**cute** Adorable. All babies are *cute.*
  cute /kūt/ *adjective*, **cuter, cutest.**

### D

**dad** Father. Children often call their father *Dad.*
  dad /dad/ *noun, plural* **dads.**
**danger** The chance that something bad or harmful will happen. The children knew the *danger* in skating on thin ice.
  dan·ger /dān′jər/ *noun, plural* **dangers.**
**dark** 1. Having little or no light. 2. Not light in color; almost the color of black.
  dark /därk/ *adjective*, **darker, darkest.**
**days** The times between sunrise and sunset.
  days /dāz/ *noun plural.*
**daze** To confuse or stun. The fall from the tree *dazed* the girl for a minute.
  daze /dāz/ *verb*, **dazed, dazing.**
**dear** 1. Much or greatly loved. Polly is my *dear* friend. 2. A much loved person. You are a *dear* to help with the party. 3. An exclamation of surprise, disappointment, or trouble. Oh *dear!* I've missed the bus.
  dear /dir/ *adjective*, **dearer, dearest;** *noun, plural* **dears;** *interjection.*
**December** The twelfth and last month.
  De·cem·ber /di sem′bər/ *noun.*
**decide** To make up one's mind.
  de·cide /di sīd′/ *verb*, **decided, deciding.**
**deep** 1. Far down from the top. She threw a penny into the *deep* well. 2. Great

in degree. She fell into a *deep* sleep. **3.** Low in pitch. He has a *deep* voice.

**deep** /dēp/ *adjective*, **deeper, deepest.**

**describe** To give a picture of something in words; tell or write about.

**de·scribe** /di skrīb'/ *verb*, **described, describing.**

**descriptive** Giving a picture in words. The tourists were given *descriptive* cards about places to visit in the city.

**de·scrip·tive** /di skrip'tiv/ *adjective*.

**dictionary** A book that has words of a language arranged in alphabetical order, together with information about them. This dictionary tells what words mean, how they are spelled, how they are used, and how they are pronounced.

**dic·tion·ar·y** /dik'shə ner ē/ *noun, plural* **dictionaries.**

**didn't** I *didn't* do my homework.

**did·n't** /did'ənt/ *contraction* for **did not.**

**different** Not alike. A bicycle and a motorcycle are *different*.

**dif·fer·ent** /dif'ər ənt/ *or* /dif'rənt/ *adjective.*

**dinosaur** One of a group of extinct reptiles that lived millions of years ago.

**di·no·saur** /dī'nə sôr'/ *noun, plural* **dinosaurs.**

**distance** The amount of space between two things or points. The *distance* from here to Jane's house is two blocks.

**dis·tance** /dis'təns/ *noun, plural* **distances.**

**divide** **1.** To separate into parts, pieces, or groups. The class *divided* into two teams. **2.** To show how many times one number contains another number.

When you *divide* 6 by 2 you get 3.

**di·vide** /di vīd'/ *verb*, **divided, dividing.**

**doctor** A person who has been trained and licensed to treat sickness or injury.

**doc·tor** /dok'tər/ *noun, plural* **doctors.**

**does** She *does* beautiful paintings.

**does** /duz/ *verb.*

**doesn't** Alan *doesn't* like cold weather.

**does·n't** /duz'ənt/ *contraction* for **does not.**

**doll** A toy that looks like a baby, a child, or a grown person.

**doll** /dol/ *noun, plural* **dolls.**

**done** **1.** The carpenters have *done* a very good job on our house. **2.** Cooked. When the meat is *done*, we can eat.

**done** /dun/ *verb; adjective.*

**donkey** An animal that looks very much like a small horse.

**don·key** /dong'kē/ *or* /dung'kē/ *noun, plural* **donkeys.**

donkey

at; āges; fäther; cär; dåring; end; mē; tėrm; it; tīger; souvenir; hot; ōld; ôff; oil; fôrk; out; up; fûll; trüly; mūsic; sing; thin; zh in treasure; ə in lemon, ago, pencil, taken, circus; ər in letter, honor, dollar.

**don't** Please *don't* tell my secret.
  **don't** /dōnt/ *contraction* for **do not.**
**down** 1. From a higher to a lower place. The painter climbed *down* the ladder. 2. Along, through, or into something. Jeff met a friend walking *down* the street.
  **down** /doun/ *adverb; preposition.*
**draw** To make a picture of something.
  **draw** /drô/ *verb,* **drew, drawn, drawing.**
**dream** A series of thoughts or feelings that a person has while asleep.
  **dream** /drēm/ *noun, plural,* **dreams.**
**dress** 1. A garment for a woman or girl that looks like a blouse and skirt sewn together. 2. To put clothes on.
  **dress** /dres/ *noun, plural* **dresses.**
**drew** Mitchell *drew* a funny picture.
  **drew** /drü/ *verb.*
**drift** 1. To move or pile up because of a current of air or water. The fisherman let his boat *drift* downstream. 2. Something that has been moved along or piled up by air or water currents. The storm caused *drifts* of snow.
  **drift** /drift/ *verb,* **drifted, drifting;** *noun, plural* **drifts.**
**drill** A tool that is used to cut holes in wood, plastic, and other hard material.
  **drill** /dril/ *noun, plural* **drills.**

drill

**drink** 1. To swallow a liquid. 2. A liquid for drinking.

**drink** /dringk/ *verb,* **drank, drunk, drinking;** *noun, plural* **drinks.**
**drive** 1. To use and steer a car or other vehicle. Dan *drove* the new tractor. 2. To go or ride in a car or other vehicle. I went on a country *drive.*
  **drive** /drīv/ *verb,* **drove, driven, driving.**
**driveway** A private road to a house, garage, or other building from a street.
  **drive·way** /drīv′wā′/ *noun, plural* **driveways.**
**drove** We *drove* downtown in the car.
  **drove** /drōv/ *verb.*
**drum** 1. A musical instrument that makes a sound when it is beaten. 2. To beat or play on a drum.
  **drum** /drum/ *noun, plural* **drums;** *verb,* **drummed, drumming.**
**dry** 1. Not wet or damp. 2. To make or become dry.
  **dry** /drī/ *adjective,* **drier, driest;** *verb,* **dried, drying.**
**during** Throughout. We go to the seashore *during* the summer.
  **dur·ing** /d(y)ėr′ing/ *preposition*

### E

**eagle** A large, powerful bird. One kind of eagle, the bald eagle, is the national symbol of the United States.
  **ea·gle** /ē′gəl/ *noun, plural* **eagles.**
**east** The direction a person faces when watching the sun rise in the morning.
  **east** /ēst/ *noun.*
**easy** Not hard to do.
  **eas·y** /ē′zē/ *adjective,* **easier, easiest.**
**eat** To chew on and swallow.
  **eat** /ēt/ *verb,* **ate, eaten, eating.**

**edit** To correct and check something written so that it is ready to be printed.
**e·dit** /ed′it/ *verb,* **edited, editing.**

**eight** One more than seven; 8.
**eight** /āt/ *noun, plural* **eights;** *adjective.*

eight

**electric** Having to do with electricity. I have a set of *electric* trains.
**e·lec·tric** /i lek′trik/ *adjective.*

**eleven** One more than ten; 11.
**e·lev·en** /i lev′ən/ *noun, plural* **elevens;** *adjective.*

**encyclopedia** A book or set of books giving a great deal of information about various subjects.
**en·cy·clo·pe·di·a** /en sī′klə pē′dē ə/ *noun, plural* **encyclopedias.**

**end** **1.** The last part. **2.** The part where something starts or stops.
**end** /end/ *noun, plural* **ends.**

**enjoy** To get joy or pleasure from; be happy with. The family *enjoys* the beach.
**en·joy** /en joi′/ *verb,* **enjoyed, enjoying.**

**enough** As much or as many as needed. There is not *enough* room for all of us in the car.
**e·nough** /i nuf′/ *adjective.*

**entire** Having all the parts; whole. Joe ate the *entire* box of crackers.
**en·tire** /en tīr′/ *adjective.*

**evening** The late afternoon and early nighttime.
**eve·ning** /ēv′ning/ *noun, plural* **evenings.**

**every** Each. *Every* boy in class is here.
**eve·ry** /ev′rē/ *adjective.*

**everyone** Each person. He bought hats for *everyone* who was at the party.
**eve·ry·one** /ev′rē wun′/ *pronoun.*

**everything** All or each thing. She showed her mother *everything* she had bought.
**eve·ry·thing** /ev′rē thing′/ *pronoun.*

**exclamation mark** A punctuation mark (!). It is used after a word, group of words, or sentence to show an exclamation of anger, surprise, or excitement. This mark of punctuation is also called an **exclamation point.**
**ex·cla·ma·tion** /eks′klə mā′shən/ **mark** (märk) *noun, plural* **marks.**

**F**

**fact** Something that is known to be true or real, that has really happened.
**fact** /fakt/ *noun, plural* **facts.**

**fall** **1.** To come down from a higher place; drop. **2.** To take place; happen. Halloween *falls* on October 31. **3.** The season between summer and winter; autumn.
**fall** /fôl/ *verb,* **fell, fallen, falling;** *noun, plural* **falls.**

at; āges; fäther; cär; dåring; end; mē; tèrm; it; tīger; souvenir; hot; ōld; ôff; oil; fôrk; out; up; fůll; trüly; mūsic; sing; thin; zh in treasure; ə in lemon, ago, pencil, taken, circus; ər in letter, honor, dollar.

**false** **1.** Not true; wrong. He gave *false* directions and the driver couldn't find his way. **2.** Not real. Her grandmother wears *false* teeth.

**false** /fôls/ *adjective*, **falser, falsest.**

**far** Not near.

**far** /fär/ *adverb*, **farther, farthest.**

**fast** **1.** Acting, moving, or done very quickly. **2.** Ahead of the correct time.

**fast** /fast/ *adjective*, **faster, fastest.**

**father** The male parent of a child.

**fa·ther** /fä′thər/ *noun, plural* **fathers.**

**fault** **1.** The responsibility for a mistake. It was her *fault* that I was late. **2.** A mistake; error. He corrected the *faults* in his spelling.

**fault** /fôlt/ *noun, plural* **faults.**

**favor** An act of kindness. He did her a *favor* by giving her a ride to school.

**fa·vor** /fā′vər/ *noun, plural* **favors.**

**feel** **1.** To find out about by touching. I can *feel* that your face is hot. **2.** To have or cause the sense of being something. I *feel* happy that I'll visit Grandpa.

**feel** /fēl/ *verb*, **felt, feeling.**

**feet** More than one foot.

**feet** /fēt/ *noun plural.*

**fern** A plant that has large feathery leaves and no flowers.

**fern** /fèrn/ *noun, plural* **ferns.**

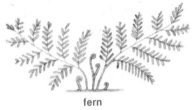

fern

**few** Not many. Only a *few* people came to the meeting.

**few** /fū/ *adjective*, **fewer, fewest.**

**find** **1.** To come upon by accident; happen on. **2.** To get or learn by adding, subtracting, multiplying, or dividing. **3.** To look for and get something lost.

**find** /fīnd/ *verb*, **found, finding.**

**fine** **1.** Of very high quality; very good. **2.** Very small; tiny. Clay is *fine* dirt.

**fine** /fīn/ *adjective*, **finer, finest;** *adverb.*

**finger** One of the five separate parts at the end of the hand. Usually, a person is said to have four fingers and a thumb.

**fin·ger** /fing′gər/ *noun, plural* **fingers.**

**first** Before all others.

**first** /fèrst/ *adjective.*

**flew** The bird *flew* up into the clouds.

**flew** /flü/ *verb.*

**flight** **1.** Movement through the air with the use of wings. We watched the graceful *flight* of the gull. **2.** A trip in an airplane. **3.** A set of stairs or steps between floors or landings of a building.

**flight** /flīt/ *noun, plural* **flights.**

**float** To rest on top of water or liquid.

**float** /flōt/ *verb*, **floated, floating.**

**food** Something that is eaten or taken in by people, animals, or plants that keeps them alive and helps them grow.

**food** /füd/ *noun, plural* **foods.**

**foot** **1.** The end part of the leg that man and other animals walk or stand on. **2.** A twelve-inch unit of measure.

**foot** /fùt/ *noun, plural* **feet.**

**footstep** A step of the foot. We all watched the baby take his first *footsteps.*

**foot·step** /fùt′step′/ *noun, plural* **footsteps.**

**for** We worked *for* two hours.

**for** /fôr/ *or* /fər/ *preposition.*

**forth**   Forward. From that day *forth*, the man was never lonely again.
   **forth** /fôrth/ *adverb.*
**four**   One more than three; 4.
   **four** /fôr/ *noun, plural* **fours;** *adjective.*
**fourth**   Next after the third.
   **fourth** /fôrth/ *adjective; noun, plural* **fourths.**
**fox**   A wild animal that is something like a dog. A fox has a pointed nose and ears, a bushy tail, and thick fur.
   **fox** /foks/ *noun, plural* **foxes.**

fox

**Friday**   The sixth day of the week.
   **Fri·day** /frī′dē/ *or* /frī′dā/ *noun, plural* **Fridays.**
**friend**   A person whom one knows and likes well.
   **friend** /frend/ *noun, plural* **friends.**
**from**   I go to school *from* nine o'clock to three.
   **from** /from/ *or* /frum/ *or* /frəm/ *preposition.*
**front**   The part that faces forward or comes first.
   **front** /frunt/ *noun, plural* **fronts.**
**full**   Holding as much or as many as possible.
   **full** /fúl/ *adjective,* **fuller, fullest.**
**fun**   Enjoyment or playfulness. We had *fun* riding our sleds down the hill.
   **fun** /fun/ *noun.*

**funny**   Causing laughter; silly. Tina told us a very *funny* joke.
   **fun·ny** /fun′ē/ *adjective,* **funnier, funniest.**
**fur**   The soft, thick hairy coat of animals like bears, cats, or rodents.
   **fur** /fėr/ *noun, plural* **furs.**

### G

**game**   A sport or contest with certain rules. Jeff likes the *game* of checkers.
   **game** /gām/ *noun, plural* **games.**
**gas**   **1.** A form of matter that is not solid or liquid. **2.** Gasoline. We filled the car's tank with *gas*.
   **gas** /gas/ *noun, plural* **gases.**
**gave**   Nancy *gave* her friend a gift.
   **gave** /gāv/ *verb.*
**geese**   More than one goose.
   **geese** /gēs/ *noun plural.*
**gem**   A precious stone that has been cut and polished; jewel. The queen wore rubies, diamonds, and other *gems*.
   **gem** /jem/ *noun, plural* **gems.**
**get**   **1.** To receive or take as one's own; gain. Alice hopes to *get* a new bicycle for her birthday. Stephen thinks he will *get* an A on the test. **2.** To cause to do, be, or become; bring about or happen. When will we *get* home? I *get* up at seven o'clock. The weather *got* very cold.
   **get** /get/ *verb,* **got, got, getting.**

at; āges; fäther; cär; dãring; end; mē; tėrm; it; tīger; souvenir; hot; ōld; ôff; oil; fôrk; out; up; fúll; trüly; mūsic; sing; thin; zh in treasure; ə in lemon, ago, pencil, taken, circus; ər in letter, honor, dollar.

**giant** **1.** An imaginary creature like a huge man. **2.** Very large.

    **gi·ant** /jī′ənt/ *noun, plural* **giants;** *adjective.*

**gift** Present. Jean could hardly wait to open her birthday *gifts.*

    **gift** /gift/ *noun, plural* **gifts.**

gift

**giraffe** A large animal that lives in Africa. The giraffe has a very long neck, long, thin legs, and a coat with brown patches. Giraffes are the tallest animals.

    **gi·raffe** /jə raf′/ *noun, plural* **giraffes.**

**girl** A female child from birth to the time she is a young woman.

    **girl** /gėrl/ *noun, plural* **girls.**

**glass** **1.** A hard material that breaks easily. Glass can be seen through. **2.** A container made of glass that is used for drinking. She filled the *glass* with milk. **3. glasses.** A pair of lenses made of glass, used to help a person see better.

    **glass** /glas/ *noun, plural* **glasses.**

**go** **1.** To move from one place to another. **2.** To pass. Time *goes* quickly.

    **go** /gō/ *verb,* **went, gone, going.**

**gold** **1.** A heavy yellow metal used to make jewelry and coins. **2.** Having the color gold. Leaves turn *gold* in the fall.

    **gold** /gōld/ *noun, plural* **golds;** *adjective.*

**good** Of high quality; not bad. I thought the movie was very *good.*

    **good** /gùd/ *adjective,* **better, best.**

**good-by** Farewell. *"Good-by!"* she called, as we drove down the driveway.

    **good-by** /gùd′bī′/ *interjection.*

**got** I *got* a new jacket last week.

    **got** /got/ *verb.*

**government** The group of people in charge of ruling a country, state, city, or other place. The *government* in this country is elected by the people.

    **gov·ern·ment** /guv′ərn mənt/ *noun, plural* **governments.**

**grade** **1.** A year or level of work in school. **2.** A number or letter showing how well a student has done in work at school; mark.

    **grade** /grād/ *noun, plural* **grades.**

**grandmother** The mother of one's mother or father.

    **grand·moth·er** /grand′mu<u>th</u>′ər/ *or* /gran′mu<u>th</u>′ər/ *noun, plural* **grandmothers.**

**grassland** Land that is covered mainly with grass and has few trees on it.

    **grass·land** /gras′land′/ *noun, plural* **grasslands.**

**great** **1.** Very large in size, number, or amount. **2.** Very important. The scientist's cure for this disease was a *great* discovery.

    **great** /grāt/ *adjective,* **greater, greatest.**

**grew** He *grew* tomatoes on his farm.

    **grew** /grü/ *verb.*

**grow** To become bigger.

    **grow** /grō/ *verb,* **grew, grown, growing.**

**guess** To form an opinion without having enough knowledge or facts to be sure. Without a watch, he could only *guess* what time it was.

    **guess** /ges/ *verb,* **guessed, guessing.**

# H

**had**  He *had* fun at the party.
**had** /had/ *verb.*

**half**  One of two equal parts of something. A pint is *half* a quart.
**half** /haf/ *noun, plural* **halves.**

**hall**  A passageway onto which rooms open in a house or other building. The students lined up in the *hall* before they went to class.
**hall** /hôl/ *noun, plural* **halls.**

**Halloween**  The evening of October 31. Halloween is celebrated by dressing up in costumes and playing tricks.
**Hal·low·een** /hal′ə wēn′/ *or* /hal′ō ēn′/ *noun, plural* **Halloweens.**

**hand**  **1.** The end part of the arm from the wrist down. It is made up of the palm, four fingers, and a thumb. **2.** To give or pass with the hand. Please *hand* me the salt.
**hand** /hand/ *noun, plural* **hands;** *verb,* **handed, handling.**

**happen**  To take place; occur. We didn't know what *happened* to the car.
**hap·pen** /hap′ən/ *verb,* **happened, happening.**

**happy**  Feeling or showing pleasure or gladness. I was *happy* at my party.
**hap·py** /hap′ē/ *adjective,* **happier, happiest.**

**harbor**  A sheltered place along a coast. Ships and boats often anchor in a harbor.
**har·bor** /här′bər/ *noun, plural* **harbors.**

**hard**  **1.** Solid and firm to the touch; not soft. Rocks are *hard.* **2.** Needing or using much effort; difficult. Chopping wood is a *hard* job.
**hard** /härd/ *adjective,* **harder, hardest.**

**has**  Betty *has* a new bicycle.
**has** /haz/ *verb.*

**hasn't**  She *hasn't* done any work at all.
**has·n't** /haz′ənt/ *contraction* for **has not.**

**have**  Do you *have* any questions? My brother might *have* the chicken pox. Mother told me I *have* to clean my room.
**have** /hav/ *verb,* **had, having.**

**haven't**  I *haven't* gone shopping yet.
**have·n't** /hav′ənt/ *contraction* for **have not.**

**hawk**  A bird of prey. It has a sharp, hooked beak, strong claws, and short rounded wings.
**hawk** /hôk/ *noun, plural* **hawks.**

hawk

**he**  Bob said that *he* would be on time.
**he** /hē/ *pronoun.*

**hear**  **1.** To receive sound through the ears. **2.** To listen to. Dad will *hear* both sides of our quarrel.
**hear** /hir/ *verb,* **heard, hearing.**

**heard**  I *heard* my brother coming in.
**heard** /hėrd/ *verb.*

at; āges; fäther; cär; dāring; end; mē; tėrm; it; tīger; souvenir; hot; ōld; ôff; oil; fôrk; out; up; fůll; trüly; mūsic; sing; thin; zh in treasure; ə in lemon, ago, pencil, taken, circus; ər in letter, honor, dollar.

**heat** **1.** The state of being hot; warmth. The *heat* of the fire warmed the whole room. **2.** To make or become hot or warm. Mom *heated* the milk before giving it to my baby sister.
   **heat** /hēt/ *noun; verb,* **heated, heating.**

**hello** A word used as a greeting.
   **hel·lo** /he lō'/ *or* /hə lō'/ *interjection.*

**help** **1.** To give or do something that is useful, wanted, or needed; aid. Barbara *helped* the blind woman across the street. **2.** To stop or avoid. I couldn't *help* laughing when I heard the story. **3.** The act of helping. Do you need *help?*
   **help** /help/ *verb,* **helped, helping;** *noun,* *plural* **helps.**

**her** I gave *her* the book. *Her* coat is on the chair. Lisa saw me with *her* brother.
   **her** /hėr/ *pronoun; adjective.*

**herd** A group of animals. A *herd* of cattle grazed in the pasture.
   **herd** /hėrd/ *noun, plural* **herds.**

**here** **1.** At, in, or to this place. I have been waiting *here* for an hour. **2.** This place. How do you get home from *here?*
   **here** /hir/ *adverb; noun.*

**he's** *He's* going to come with us.
   **he's** /hēz/ *contraction* for **he is** and **he has.**

**hidden** The dog has *hidden* his bone.
   **hid·den** /hid'ən/ *verb.*

**high** **1.** Tall. **2.** Shrill; sharp. The soprano sang a *high* note.
   **high** /hī/ *adjective,* **higher, highest.**

**higher** Taller than. This shelf is *higher* than that one.
   **high·er** /hī'ər/ *adjective.*

**him** We saw *him* yesterday at the game.
   **him** /him/ *or* /im/ *pronoun.*

**himself** Tom ties his shoes *himself.*
   **him·self** /him self'/ *pronoun.*

**his** This is my book and that one is *his.* *His* dog has floppy ears.
   **his** /hiz/ *pronoun; adjective.*

**hole** **1.** A hollow place in something solid. **2.** An opening through something. I wore a *hole* in my old sweater.
   **hole** /hōl/ *noun, plural* **holes.**

**home** The place in which a person or animal lives. A nest is a bird's *home.*
   **home** /hōm/ *noun, plural* **homes.**

**honeycomb** A wax structure made by bees to store their honey in, with layers of six-sided cells.
   **hon·ey·comb** /hun'ē kōm'/ *noun, plural* **honeycombs.**

honeycomb

**hood** **1.** A covering for the head and neck. A hood is often attached to the collar of a coat. **2.** The metal cover that is over the engine of an automobile.
   **hood** /hud/ *noun, plural* **hoods.**

**hope** To want or wish for something very much. I *hope* Susan will be better.
   **hope** /hōp/ *verb,* **hoped, hoping.**

**horse** A large animal with four legs with hooves and a long, flowing mane and tail.
   **horse** /hôrs/ *noun, plural* **horses.**

**hour** Sixty minutes. We waited for one *hour*, from four o'clock to five o'clock, for Tom to meet us.
   **hour** /our/ *noun, plural* **hours.**

**house** A building in which people live; home. We went over to Dave's *house*.
**house** /hous/ *noun*, *plural* **houses.**

house

**how** *How* cold is it outside? *How* did you like the movie?
**how** /hou/ *adverb*.

**huge** Very big. Whales are *huge* animals.
**huge** /hūj/ *adjective*, **huger, hugest.**

**hundred** Ten times ten; 100.
**hun·dred** /hun'drid/ *noun*, *plural* **hundreds;** *adjective.*

**hurry** To move faster than is usual; rush. We must *hurry* to catch the bus.
**hur·ry** /hėr'ē/ *verb*, **hurried, hurrying.**

**hurt** **1.** To cause pain or injury. He fell and *hurt* his arm. She *hurt* his feelings when she laughed at him. **2.** To be bad for; harm. Being sick so often *hurt* his chances of making the team.
**hurt** /hėrt/ *verb*, **hurt, hurting.**

**I**

**I** *I* call myself me.
**I** /ī/ *pronoun.*

**ideal** A person or thing thought of as being perfect.
**i·de·al** /ī dē'əl/ *noun*, *plural* **ideals.**

**I'll** *I'll* go if you will.
**I'll** /īl/ *contraction* for **I will** and **I shall.**

**I'm** *I'm* going to the zoo today.

**I'm** /īm/ *contraction* for **I am.**

**in** The cat is *in* the house. Please come *in* out of the cold.
**in** /in/ *preposition; adverb.*

**inch** 1/12th of a foot. Twelve inches equals one foot.
**inch** /inch/ *noun*, *plural* **inches.**

**inn** A small hotel.
**inn** /in/ *noun*, *plural* **inns.**

**inside** **1.** The inner side or part. **2.** Indoors. **3.** In or into the inside of. I looked *inside* the closet for my coat.
**in·side** /in'sīd'/ *or* /in'sīd'/ *for noun and adjective;* /in'sīd'/ *for adverb and preposition; noun*, *plural* **insides;** *adjective; adverb; preposition.*

**instead** In place of another person or thing. We asked her brother to come to the movies, but she came *instead*.
**in·stead** /in sted'/ *adverb.*

**interesting** Causing or holding interest or attention.
**in·ter·est·ing** /in'tə res'ting/ *or* /in'tris ting/ *adjective.*

**is** She *is* not home. Today *is* Friday.
**is** /iz/ *verb.*

**isn't** She *isn't* home yet.
**is·n't** /iz'ənt/ *contraction* for **is not.**

**it** *It* snowed last night. Give *it* to me.
**it** /it/ *pronoun.*

**its** The cat licked *its* paw.
**its** /its/ *adjective.*

at; āges; fäther; cär; dāring; end; mē; tėrm; it; tīger; souvenir; hot; ōld; ôff; oil; fôrk; out; up; fùll; trüly; mūsic; sing; thin; zh in treasure; ə in lemon, ago, pencil, taken, circus; ər in letter, honor, dollar.

**it's** *It's* cold today. *It's* been nice to see you. *It's* not the right house.

   **it's** /its/ *contraction* for **it is** and **it has.**

**I've** *I've* been home all day.

   **I've** /īv/ *contraction* for **I have.**

## J

**jean** **1.** A strong cotton cloth used to make work clothes and other kinds of sport clothes. **2. jeans.** Trousers or over-alls made out of this cloth.

   **jean** /jēn/ *noun, plural* **jeans.**

**jerk** A sudden, sharp pull or twist. Joe gave the rope a *jerk.*

   **jerk** /jėrk/ *noun, plural* **jerks.**

**jet** A plane driven by a stream of hot gas.

   **jet** /jet/ *noun, plural* **jets.**

**job** **1.** A position of work. **2.** Something that has to be done.

   **job** /job/ *noun, plural* **jobs.**

**join** **1.** To put together to make one. Joan tied a knot to *join* the two ends of the rope. **2.** To become a member of. Bill *joined* the Boy Scouts.

   **join** /join/ *verb,* **joined, joining.**

**jolly** Full of fun; merry.

   **jol·ly** /jol′ē/ *adjective,* **jollier, jolliest.**

**joy** A strong feeling of happiness.

   **joy** /joi/ *noun, plural* **joys.**

**July** The seventh month of the year.

   **Ju·ly** /jü lī′/ *noun.*

**jungle** Land in tropical areas that is covered with a thick mass of trees, vines, and bushes.

   **jun·gle** /jung′gəl/ *noun, plural* **jungles.**

**just** **1.** Exactly. You said *just* what I was going to say. **2.** A little while ago. I *just* saw your book on the table. **3.** By very little. Bob *just* got to school in time.

   **just** /just/ *adverb.*

## K

**kangaroo** An Australian animal that has small front legs and very strong back legs, which it uses for leaping. A female kangaroo carries her young in a pouch for about six months after birth.

   **kan·ga·roo** /kang′gə rü′/ *noun, plural* **kangaroos** or **kangaroo.**

kangaroo

**keep** **1.** To continue to have, hold, or do. Mother let her *keep* the kitten. **2.** To store or put. Jerry *keeps* his toys in the closet. **3.** To be faithful to. The boy *kept* his promise and mowed the lawn.

   **keep** /kēp/ *verb,* **kept, keeping.**

**kind** **1.** Gentle, friendly. **2.** A type or class. The whale is a *kind* of mammal.

   **kind** /kīnd/ *adjective,* **kinder, kindest;** *noun, plural* **kinds.**

**king** A man who rules a country.

   **king** /king/ *noun, plural* **kings.**

**kitten** A young cat.

   **kit·ten** /kit′ən/ *noun, plural* **kittens.**

**knee** The joint of the leg between the thigh and the lower leg.

   **knee** /nē/ *noun, plural* **knees.**

**knew** Sally *knew* the right answer.

**knew** /nü/ *or* /nū/ *verb.*

**knife** A tool with a sharp blade attached to a handle used for cutting.
**knife** /nīf/ *noun, plural* **knives.**

**knit** To make by looping yarn together. The woman was *knitting* a sweater.
**knit** /nit/ *verb,* **knitted** or **knit, knitting.**

**knock** **1.** To strike with a sharp, hard blow or blows; hit. **2.** To push and cause to fall.
**knock** /nok/ *verb,* **knocked, knocking.**

**knot** **1.** A fastening made by tying together pieces of thread, string, or cord. **2.** A tangle or lump.
**knot** /not/ *noun, plural* **knots.**

**know** **1.** To understand clearly. **2.** To be familiar with.
**know** /nō/ *verb,* **knew, known, knowing.**

**known** It is *known* that Christopher Columbus first reached America in 1492.
**known** /nōn/ *verb.*

**L**

**lady** Any woman. "There is a *lady* at the door to see you," Mark said.
**la·dy** /lā'dē/ *noun, plural* **ladies.**

**lamb** A young sheep.
**lamb** /lam/ *noun, plural* **lambs.**

lamb

**landform** A feature on the surface of the earth, like a valley or a mountain.
**land·form** /land'fôrm/ *noun.*

**language** **1.** Spoken or written words. **2.** The speech of a country or group. The *language* of Mexico is Spanish.
**lan·guage** /lang'gwij/ *noun, plural* **languages.**

**large** Big in size or amount; huge.
**large** /lärj/ *adjective,* **larger, largest.**

**late** **1.** Coming after the usual time. **2.** Coming near the end. It was *late* in the afternoon when we started our trip.
**late** /lāt/ *adjective,* **later, latest.**

**lawn** An area with mowed grass around a house or other building.
**lawn** /lôn/ *noun, plural* **lawns.**

**leaf** A flat, green part of a plant.
**leaf** /lēf/ *noun, plural* **leaves.**

**left** **1.** On the west side of your body when you face north. Carl writes with his *left* hand. **2.** The *left* side. His brother is standing on his *left* in the photograph. **3.** Toward the left. Turn *left* at the next corner. **4.** To leave behind. I *left* it home.
**left** /left/ *adjective; noun; adverb; verb.*

**less** A smaller amount. Ed has *less* work to do today than he had yesterday.
**less** /les/ *adjective.*

**lesson** Something that is learned or to be learned. What words are in the *lesson?*
**les·son** /les'ən/ *noun, plural* **lessons.**

at; āges; fäther; cär; dåring; end; mē; tèrm; it; tīger; souvenir; hot; ōld; ôff; oil; fôrk; out; up; full; trüly; mūsic; sing; thin; zh in treasure; ə in lemon, ago, pencil, taken, circus; ər in letter, honor, dollar.

**let's**   *Let's* go for a walk.
 **let's** /lets/ *contraction* for **let us.**
**letter**   **1.** A mark that stands for a speech sound. The word "run" has three *letters.* **2.** A written message. Philip mailed a *letter* to his friend.
 **let·ter** /let'ər/ *noun, plural* **letters.**
**lift**   To raise; pick up. I can't *lift* this heavy suitcase.
 **lift** /lift/ *verb,* **lifted, lifting.**
**lion**   A large, strong animal of the cat family. A lioness is a female *lion.*
 **li·on** /lī'ən/ *noun, plural* **lions.**

lion

**little**   **1.** Small in size or amount. A pebble is a *little* stone. **2.** Short in time or distance. We will be home in a *little* while. **3.** A small amount. I ate only a *little.*
 **lit·tle** /lit'əl/ *adjective,* **less** or **lesser** or **littler, least** or **littlest;** *noun.*
**loose**   **1.** Not fastened or attached firmly. A page was *loose* in the book. **2.** Free. The canary is *loose* in the house. **3.** Not tight. He wore a *loose* jacket.
 **loose** /lüs/ *adjective,* **looser, loosest.**
**lose**   **1.** To have no longer; be without. The family will *lose* all their belongings if the firemen can't save their house. I *lost* my pencil. **2.** To fail to keep. He *loses* his temper easily. **3.** To fail to win. The team *lost* the game.
 **lose** /lüz/ *verb,* **lost, losing.**

**lot**   **1.** A plot of land. We play baseball on an empty *lot.* **2.** A great amount. There are a *lot* of cars on the street.
 **lot** /lot/ *noun, plural* **lots.**
**loud**   Having a strong sound; not quiet. The jet plane made a *loud* noise.
 **loud** /loud/ *adjective,* **louder, loudest.**
**low**   **1.** Not high or tall. The branches of the tree are *low* enough for me to reach. **2.** Below the usual level. The river was *low.* **3.** Not having enough. Our car is *low* on gasoline. **4.** Not loud; soft. He spoke in a *low* voice.
 **low** /lō/ *adjective,* **lower, lowest.**
**lower**   **1.** Beneath a certain level. He lives on a *lower* floor of the apartment house. **2.** To take down; bring down. The boys will *lower* the flag at dusk. **3.** To make less; lessen. *Lower* your voice.
 **low·er** /lō'ər/ *adjective; verb,* **lowered, lowering.**
**lung**   One of two organs for breathing in the chest of man and other animals.
 **lung** /lung/ *noun, plural* **lungs.**

**M**

**made**   Tom *made* a map of his town.
 **made** /mād/ *verb.*
**mail**   **1.** Letters, packages, and papers that are sent or received through the post office. **2.** To send by mail.
 **mail** /māl/ *noun, plural* **mails;** *verb,* **mailed, mailing.**
**manner**   **1.** A way of acting or behaving. The old woman had a warm and friendly *manner.* **2. manners.** Polite ways of behaving or acting.
 **man·ner** /man'ər/ *noun, plural* **manners.**

**many**  Made up of a large number. There are *many* books on history.
  **man·y** /men′ē/ *adjective,* **more, most.**

**may**  *May* I borrow your bicycle? Yes, you *may.*
  **may** /mā/ *verb.*

**maybe**  Perhaps, could be. I don't agree with you, but *maybe* you are right.
  **may·be** /mā′bē/ *adverb.*

**mayor**  The person who is the official head of a city or town government.
  **may·or** /mā′ər/ *noun, plural* **mayors.**

**me**  My friend sent *me* a birthday card.
  **me** /mē/ *pronoun.*

**meet**  **1.** To come face to face with. While walking down town, Bill and Jane *meet* a friend. **2.** To keep an appointment with. Jack asked Robin to *meet* him outside of school at three o'clock.
  **meet** /mēt/ *verb,* **met, meeting.**

**melt**  To change from a solid to a liquid by heating. The warm sun *melted* the ice.
  **melt** /melt/ *verb,* **melted, melting.**

**merry**  Cheerful; full of fun; jolly.
  **mer·ry** /mer′ē/ *adjective,* **merrier, merriest.**

**mile**  A measure of distance equal to 5,280 feet. Walking a *mile* made me tired.
  **mile** /mīl/ *noun, plural* **miles.**

**mind**  **1.** The part of a person that thinks, knows, learns, remembers, understands, and feels. Keep your *mind* on what you are doing. **2.** To pay attention to. *Mind* your manners. **3.** To take care of. The baby-sitter *minds* us when our parents go out. **4.** Not to like something. Do you *mind* going to the movies?
  **mind** /mīnd/ *noun, plural* **minds;** *verb,* **minded, minding.**

**minute**  **1.** Sixty seconds. There are sixty minutes in an hour. **2.** A moment in time; instant. See you in a *minute.*
  **min·ute** /min′it/ *noun, plural* **minutes.**

**mitten**  A warm covering for the hand. A mitten covers four fingers together and the thumb separately.
  **mit·ten** /mit′n/ *noun, plural* **mittens.**

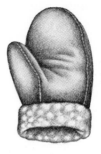

mitten

**mix**  **1.** To put two or more different things together. **2.** Something that is made by mixing; mixture.
  **mix** /miks/ *verb,* **mixed, mixing;** *noun, plural* **mixes.**

**modern**  Having to do with the present time. Computers are *modern* inventions.
  **mod·ern** /mod′ərn/ *adjective.*

**Monday**  The second day of the week.
  **Mon·day** /mun′dē/ *or* /mun′dā/ *noun, plural* **Mondays.**

**money**  The coins and paper currency of a country. Can you spend the *money?*
  **mon·ey** /mun′ē/ *noun, plural* **moneys.**

at; āges; fäther; cär; daring; end; mē; tėrm; it; tīger; souvenir; hot; ōld; ôff; oil; fôrk; out; up; füll; trüly; mūsic; sing; thin; zh in treasure; ə in lemon, ago, pencil, taken, circus; ər in letter, honor, dollar.

**monument** A building, statue, or other object that is made to honor a person or event. The Washington *Monument* was built in honor of George Washington.
**mon·u·ment** /mon'yə mənt/ *noun, plural* **monuments.**

**moon** A heavenly body that goes around the earth.
**moon** /mün/ *noun, plural* **moons.**

**morning** The first part of the day. Morning ends at noon.
**morn·ing** /môr'ning/ *noun, plural* **mornings.**

**most** 1. Greatest in number, amount, or degree. Who received the *most* votes? 2. Nearly all. *Most* children like games. 3. To the greatest degree. That was the *most* interesting book I have ever read.
**most** /mōst/ *adjective, adverb.*

**mother** The female parent of a child.
**moth·er** /mu<u>th</u>'ər/ *noun, plural* **mothers.**

**mouse** A small, furry animal with a pointed nose and a long, thin tail.
**mouse** /mous/ *noun, plural* **mice.**

**much** 1. Great in amount or degree. We had too *much* rain this week. 2. Very. We weren't *much* happy about the rain.
**much** /much/ *adjective,* **more, most;** *adverb,* **more, most.**

**mud** Soft, wet, sticky earth or dirt. We tracked *mud* in the house after it rained.
**mud** /mud/ *noun.*

**mule** An animal that is produced by a female horse and a male donkey.
**mule** /mūl/ *noun, plural* **mules.**

**multiply** To add a number to itself a certain number of times. If we *multiply* 2 times 4, we get 8.

**mul·ti·ply** /mul'tə plī'/ *verb,* **multiplied, multiplying.**

**museum** A building where objects of art, science, or history are kept and displayed for people to see.
**mu·se·um** /mū zē'əm/ *noun, plural* **museums.**

**must** Have to. You *must* return a book you borrow. People *must* eat to live.
**must** /must/ *verb.*

**my** Alan is *my* brother. That is *my* pen.
**my** /mī/ *adjective.*

**N**

**name** The word or words by which a person, animal, place, or thing is known. Her *name* is Debbie Taylor.
**name** /nām/ *noun, plural* **names.**

**napkin** A piece of cloth or paper used at meals for protecting clothing and for wiping the lips and hands.
**nap·kin** /nap'kin/ *noun, plural* **napkins.**

**new** Recently grown or made; not old.
**new** /nü/ or /nū/ *adjective,* **newer, newest.**

**nice** 1. Pleasant or agreeable. Today the weather is *nice.* 2. Kind and thoughtful. Julie was *nice* to invite us.
**nice** /nīs/ *adjective,* **nicer, nicest.**

**night** The time when it is dark; time between sunset and sunrise.
**night** /nīt/ *noun, plural* **nights.**

night

**no** *No*, I don't want any more milk. There were *no* mistakes in her test.
**no** /nō/ *adverb; adjective.*

**noise** **1.** A sound that is loud or harsh. **2.** Any sound. The *noise* woke us up.
**noise** /noiz/ *noun, plural* **noises.**

**none** Not any. All the boys tried to catch the rabbit, but *none* were that fast.
**none** /nun/ *pronoun.*

**normal** Like most others; regular. A *normal* temperature is 98.6 degrees.
**nor·mal** /nôr′məl/ *adjective.*

**noun** A word that names a person, place, or thing. Such words as *Mary, child, river, house,* and *courage* are nouns.
**noun** /noun/ *noun, plural* **nouns.**

**November** The eleventh month.
**No·vem·ber** /nō vem′bər/ *noun.*

**now** At the present time. I really have to go *now*. Bob should be home by *now*.
**now** /nou/ *adverb; conjunction; noun.*

**number** **1.** The total amount of things in a group; how many there are of something. The *number* of children in our family is three. **2.** A symbol or word that tells how many or which one. 2, 5, 77, and 396 are *numbers.*
**num·ber** /num′bər/ *noun, plural* **numbers.**

## O

**octopus** An animal that lives in salt water and has a soft, rounded body and eight arms. There are suckers on the arms to help the octopus move along the ocean bottom and catch food.
**oc·to·pus** /ok′tə pəs/ *noun, plural* **octopuses.**

**off** He took the book *off* the shelf. Please turn the radio *off*. Father took the day *off* to see us. The lights in the house are *off*.
**off** /ôf/ *preposition; adverb; adjective.*

**often** Many times. We went swimming *often* this summer.
**of·ten** /ô′fən/ *adverb.*

**on** Your coat is *on* the bed. Harry is *on* the team. Turn the water *on*. The radio is *on*.
**on** /ôn/ *or* /on/ *preposition; adverb; adjective.*

**once** **1.** One time. He has a piano lesson *once* a week. **2.** In time past; before. Parents were *once* children. **3.** As soon as; when. The game is easy, *once* you learn the rules.
**once** /wuns/ *adverb; conjunction.*

**one** **1.** The first and lowest number; 1. **2.** A single person or thing.
**one** /wun/ *noun, plural* **ones.**

**open** **1.** Not shut. The bird flew in an *open* window. **2.** To make or become open. She *opened* the envelope.
**o·pen** /ō′pən/ *adjective; verb,* **opened, opening.**

open

at; āges; fäther; cär; dãring; end; mē; tėrm; it; tīger; souvenir; hot; ōld; ôff; oil; fôrk; out; up; fùll; trüly; mūsic; sing; thin; zh in treasure; ə in lemon, ago, pencil, taken, circus; ər in letter, honor, dollar.

**opinion**   A belief that is based on what a person thinks, rather than on what is proved or known to be true. It is my *opinion* that he will win the race.
   **o·pin·ion** /ə pin′yən/ *noun, plural* **opinions.**

**or**   Is your new coat blue *or* green?
   **or** /ôr/ *conjunction.*

**orchard**   Where fruit trees are grown.
   **or·chard** /ôr′chərd/ *noun, plural* **orchards.**

orchard

**order**   **1.** A command to do something. **2.** The way in which things are arranged. She called the names in ABC *order.* **3.** Clean, neat, or proper condition. Tom kept his room in *order.* **4.** A request for goods. Father gave the waiter our *order.*
   **or·der** /ôr′dər/ *noun, plural* **orders.**

**our**   That is *our* dog.
   **our** /our/ *adjective.*

**out**   The firemen put *out* the fire. Watch *out* for the car. The dress is made *out* of silk. She looked *out* the window.
   **out** /out/ *adverb; adjective; preposition.*

**outside**   **1.** The outer side, surface, or part. The *outside* of the house was painted **2.** On the outside; outer. The *outside* layer of paint was peeling. **3.** On or to the outside; outdoors. Do you want to go *outside* for some fresh air?
   **out·side** /out′sīd′/ *or* /out′sīd′/ *noun, plural* **outsides;** *adjective; adverb.*

**over**   The horse jumped *over* the fence. The summer will soon be *over.*
   **o·ver** /ō′vər/ *preposition; adverb.*

**owl**   A bird that has a round head with large staring eyes and a hooked bill, a short square tail, and soft feathers.
   **owl** /oul/ *noun, plural* **owls.**

**own**   **1.** The accident was her *own* fault. **2.** That bicycle is my *own.* **3.** That farmer *owns* two tractors.
   **own** /ōn/ *adjective; noun; verb,* **owned, owning.**

## P

**page**   One side of a sheet of paper in a book, newspaper, or magazine.
   **page** /pāj/ *noun, plural* **pages.**

**paid**   He *paid* his friend a visit. She *paid* the gas bill.
   **paid** /pād/ *verb.*

**paint**   **1.** Matter with color used with a brush. **2.** To put on colored matter with a brush. The workers *paint* the house.
   **paint** /pānt/ *noun, plural* **paints;** *verb,* **painted, painting.**

**paragraph**   A group of sentences on one particular subject or idea.
   **par·a·graph** /par′ə graf′/ *noun, plural* **paragraphs.**

**part**   **1.** Something less than the whole. Jack ate only *part* of his dinner. **2.** A share. We each did our *part.* **3.** A character in a movie or play. Neil had the *part* of a cowboy in the play.
   **part** /pärt/ *noun, plural* **parts.**

**party**   A gathering of people to have a good time. The birthday *party* was fun.
   **par·ty** /pär′tē/ *noun, plural* **parties.**

**path**   A trail or way on which people or

animals may walk.

**path** /path/ *noun, plural* **paths.**

**paw**   The foot of a four-footed animal having nails or claws.

**paw** /pô/ *noun, plural* **paws.**

**peace**   1. Freedom from fighting. The conference was held to work toward world *peace.* 2. A lack of noise; quiet or calm. He loves the *peace* of the country.

**peace** /pēs/ *noun.*

**penny**   A coin that is worth one cent.

**pen·ny** /pen′ē/ *noun, plural* **pennies.**

**people**   Men, women, and children.

**peo·ple** /pē′pəl/ *noun, plural* **people.**

**period**   A mark of punctuation (.). The period shows the end of a sentence or of an abbreviation (Ms., Mon., N.J.).

**per·i·od** /pēr′ē əd/ *noun, plural* **periods.**

**piece**   A part broken, cut, or torn from something. *Pieces* of glass are on the floor.

**piece** /pēs/ *noun, plural* **pieces.**

**pigeon**   A bird that has a plump body, a small head, and thick soft feathers.

**pi·geon** /pij′ən/ *noun, plural* **pigeons.**

pigeon

**pink**   1. A light red color, made with red and white. 2. Having the color pink.

**pink** /pingk/ *noun; adjective,* **pinker, pinkest.**

**pirate**   A person who robs ships at sea.

**pi·rate** /pī′rit/ *noun, plural* **pirates.**

**plain**   1. Clearly seen, heard, or understood. 2. Without decoration. 3. Not rich or highly seasoned. 4. An open area of flat land.

**plain** /plān/ *adjective,* **plainer, plainest;** *noun, plural* **plains.**

**plate**   1. A flat or shallow dish. Food is served or eaten from *plates.* 2. Home plate in a baseball game.

**plate** /plāt/ *noun, plural* **plates.**

**play**   1. A story that is written to be acted out on a stage. 2. A move or turn in a game. 3. To do something for fun. 4. To make music. I can *play* the piano.

**play** /plā/ *noun, plural* **plays;** *verb,* **played, playing.**

**playtime**   A time for play or recreation.

**play·time** /plā′tīm/ *noun, plural* **playtimes.**

**please**   1. To give pleasure to. 2. *Please* is also used to ask politely for something. Close the door, *please.*

**please** /plēz/ *verb,* **pleased, pleasing.**

**point**   1. A fine, sharp end. You write with the *point* of your pencil. 2. A dot; mark. A period is a *point.* 3. The main part, idea, or purpose. What is the *point* of that joke? 4. A score in a game. Our football team is ahead by six *points.* 5. To show. Tim *pointed* at the bicycle.

**point** /point/ *noun, plural* **points;** *verb,* **pointed, pointing.**

at; āges; fäther; cär; dåring; end; mē; tėrm; it; tīger; souvenir; hot; ōld; ôff; oil; fôrk; out; up; fůll; trüly; mūsıc; sing; thin; zh in treasure; ə in lemon, ago, pencil, taken, circus; ər in letter, honor, dollar.

**pool**　A tank of water to swim in. Pools can be either indoors or outdoors.
　**pool** /pül/ *noun, plural* **pools.**

**popcorn**　A kind of corn having kernels that burst open with a pop when heated. The kernels become white and fluffy, and can be eaten.
　**pop·corn** /pop'kôrn'/ *noun.*

**poppy**　A plant with round, red or yellow flowers.
　**pop·py** /pop'ē/ *noun, plural* **poppies.**

**porcupine**　An animal whose body is covered with sharp quills. It belongs to the rodent family.
　**por·cu·pine** /pôr'kyə pīn'/ *noun, plural* **porcupines.**

porcupine

**possessive**　A word showing that something belongs to someone.
　**pos·ses·sive** /pə zes'iv/ *adjective, noun, plural* **possessives.**

**predicate**　The part of a sentence that shows what the subject is or what the subject does.
　**pred·i·cate** /pred'i kit/ *noun, plural* **predicates.**

**prefix**　A syllable or group of syllables added to the front of the word. A prefix can change the meaning of the word or form a new word.
　**pre·fix** /pre'fiks/ *noun, plural* **prefixes.**

**price**　The amount of money for which something is bought or sold; cost.
　**price** /prīs/ *noun, plural* **prices.**

**probably**　Most likely. We will *probably* go on a trip this summer.
　**prob·a·bly** /prob'ə blē/ *adverb.*

**proper noun**　Having to do with a particular person, place, or thing. A *proper noun* usually begins with a capital letter. *Mary, Friday,* and *Boston* are *proper nouns.*
　**prop·er** /prop'ər/ *adjective;*
　**noun** /noun/ *noun, plural* **nouns.**

**pull**　**1.** To grab or hold something and move it forward or toward oneself. **2.** To remove or tear out something.
　**pull** /pùl/ *verb,* **pulled, pulling.**

**pulley**　A wheel with a groove around it that a rope or chain can be pulled over. Pulleys are used to lift heavy weights.
　**pul·ley** /pùl'ē/ *noun, plural* **pulleys.**

**purple**　**1.** The color made by mixing red and blue. **2.** Having the color purple.
　**pur·ple** /pėr'pəl/ *noun, plural* **purples;** *adjective.*

**put**　To cause something to be in a certain place. *Put* the box on the table.
　**put** /pùt/ *verb,* **put, putting.**

**q**

**quart**　A unit of measure. It is equal to two pints or four cups.
　**quart** /kwôrt/ *noun, plural* **quarts.**

**quarter**　**1.** One of four equal parts. **2.** A coin equal to twenty-five cents or one-quarter of a dollar.
　**quar·ter** /kwôr'tər/ *noun, plural* **quarter.**

**queen**　**1.** The wife or widow of a king. **2.** A woman who rules a kingdom.
　**queen** /kwēn/ *noun, plural* **queens.**

**question mark**　A punctuation mark

(?) that is put at the end of a question.
**ques·tion** /kwes′chən/ *noun.*
**mark** /märk/ *noun, plural* **marks.**

**quick** Happening in a short time; fast. Leslie made a *quick* trip to the store.
**quick** /kwik/ *adjective,* **quicker, quickest.**

**quiet** Making little or no noise; peaceful. It is always *quiet* in the library.
**qui·et** /kwī′it/ *adjective,* **quieter, quietest.**

**quilt** A bed covering made of two pieces of cloth that are stuffed with soft material. The two pieces of cloth are held together by lines of stitching that are sewn all over the surface of the cloth.
**quilt** /kwilt/ *noun, plural* **quilts.**

**quit** To stop doing something.
**quit** /kwit/ *verb,* **quit** or **quitted, quitting.**

**quite** **1.** Very much or completely. It is *quite* warm today. **2.** Really. Climbing the mountain was *quite* an achievement.
**quite** /kwīt/ *adverb.*

### R

**rabbit** A small animal that has long ears, a short tail, and soft fur. It belongs to the rodent family.
**rab·bit** /rab′it/ *noun, plural* **rabbits.**

**rag** A small piece of cloth, usually of worn or torn material.
**rag** /rag/ *noun, plural* **rags.**

**rain** Water that falls in drops from clouds to the earth.
**rain** /rān/ *noun, plural* **rains.**

**rainfall** The amount of rain, snow, sleet, or hail that falls on an area in a certain period of time.

**rain·fall** /rān′fôl′/ *noun, plural* **rainfalls.**

rainfall

**read** To look at and understand something that is written.
**read** /rēd/ *verb,* **read** /red/, **reading.**

**reader** **1.** A person who reads. **2.** A schoolbook that helps to teach reading.
**read·er** /rē′dər/ *noun, plural* **readers.**

**ready** **1.** Prepared for use or action. **2.** Willing.
**read·y** /red′ē/ *adjective,* **readier, readiest.**

**real** **1.** True. The man's story was *real*; he did not make it up. **2.** Not fake. These flowers are *real*, not plastic.
**re·al** /rē′əl/ *or* /rēl/ *adjective.*

**really** **1.** In fact; actually. **2.** Truly; very. Susan *really* liked the park.
**re·al·ly** /rē′ə lē/ *or* /rē′lē/ *adverb.*

**remember** **1.** To bring back or recall to the mind. **2.** To keep in mind carefully.
**re·mem·ber** /ri mem′bər/ *verb,* **remembered, remembering.**

at; āges; fäther; cär; dãring; end; mē; tėrm; it; tīger; souvenir; hot; ōld; ôff; oil; fôrk; out; up; fůll; trůly; mūsiç; sing; thin; zh in treasure; ə in lemon, ago, pencil, taken, circus; ər in letter, honor, dollar.

**reservation** Land set aside by the government for a special purpose. Reservations have been set aside for Indian tribes to live on. Places where wild animals can live without danger of being killed are called reservations.

**res·er·va·tion** /rez′ər vā′shən/ *noun, plural* **reservations.**

**ribbon** A band of cloth, paper, or other material that is used for decoration.

**rib·bon** /rib′ən/ *noun, plural* **ribbons.**

**right** 1. Correct or true. She gave the *right* answer. 2. On or toward the side of the body that is to the east when one is facing north. He writes with his *right* hand. 3. Without delay; immediately. Let's leave *right* after breakfast.

**right** /rīt/ *adjective; adverb.*

**road** A strip of cleared ground used for going from one place to another.

**road** /rōd/ *noun, plural* **roads.**

**room** 1. An area that is or may be taken up by something. There was no *room* to park the car. 2. An area in a house or other building that is separated or set off by walls. Our house has seven *rooms.*

**room** /rüm/ *or* /rùm/ *noun, plural* **rooms.**

**rooster** A male chicken.

**roost·er** /rüs′tər/ *noun, plural* **roosters.**

rooster

**root** The lower part of a plant that grows down into the ground.

**root** /rüt/ *noun, plural* **roots.**

**round** 1. Shaped like a ball or globe. Grapefuits are *round*. 2. Around. The top spun *round* and *round*.

**round** /round/ *adjective,* **rounder, roundest;** *adverb; preposition.*

**rub** 1. To press along; put pressure on the surface of. 2. Apply pressure in order to clean, polish, or make smooth.

**rub** /rub/ *verb,* **rubbed, rubbing.**

**run** To go quickly; to move faster than a walk. Mother must *run* to get the bus.

**run** /run/ *verb,* **ran, run, running.**

**s**

**said** Say earlier. Lucy *said* "hello" to the mail carrier yesterday.

**said** /sed/ *verb.*

**sail** 1. A piece of material that is attached to a boat or ship, used to catch the wind and move the boat forward in the water. 2. A trip or ride in a sail boat. 3. To move through or over the water.

**sail** /sāl/ *noun, plural* **sails;** *verb,* **sailed, sailing.**

**sailor** A person whose work is sailing a boat. A sailor may work for a steamship company or be in the navy.

**sail·or** /sā′lər/ *noun, plural* **sailors.**

**sale** 1. An exchange of goods or property for money. 2. Selling something for less than it usually costs.

**sale** /sāl/ *noun, plural* **sales.**

**salt** A white substance that is found in sea water and in the earth. Salt is used to season and preserve foods.

**salt** /sôlt/ *noun, plural* **salts.**

**sand** Tiny loose grains of crushed or worn-down rocks. Sand is found on beaches and deserts.
**sand** /sand/ *noun.*

**Saturday** The seventh day of the week.
**Sat·ur·day** /sat′ər dē/ *or* /sat′ər dā′/ *noun, plural* **Saturdays.**

**saw** 1. A tool or machine that has a sharp metal blade with teeth on one edge. It is used for cutting wood, metal, or other hard materials. 2. To cut or be cut with a saw. 3. To have seen.
**saw** /sô/ *noun, plural* **saws;** *verb,* **sawed, sawing.**

**says** Janet *says* she doesn't want to go.
**says** /sez/ *verb.*

**scale** 1. A device used to find out how heavy something is. 2. One of the hard, flat structures that cover the body of fish, snakes, and lizards.
**scale** /skāl/ *noun, plural* **scales.**

scale

**scare** To frighten or become afraid.
**scare** /skãr/ *verb,* **scared, scaring.**

**school** 1. A place for teaching and learning. 2. A group of water animals swimming together.
**school** /skül/ *noun, plural* **schools.**

**schoolyard** A yard of a school.
**school·yard** /skül′·yard/ *noun, plural* **schoolyards**

**seal** A sea animal that lives in cold re-gions and has flippers instead of feet.
**seal** /sēl/ *noun, plural* **seals** or **seal.**

**seashore** The land near or on the sea.
**sea·shore** /sē′shôr′/ *noun, plural* **sea-shores.**

**second** 1. Next after the first. 2. One of sixty parts of a minute.
**sec·ond** /sek′ənd/ *adjective; noun, plural* **seconds.**

**see** To look at with the eyes.
**see** /sē/ *verb,* **saw, seen, seeing.**

**seem** To appear to be. The tall boy *seems* older than he really is.
**seem** /sēm/ *verb,* **seemed, seeming.**

**send** To cause to go from one place to another. Mary *sends* cards to Ed.
**send** /send/ *verb,* **sent, sending.**

**sent** Edna *sent* a package to her uncle.
**sent** /sent/ *verb.*

**sentence** A group of words that gives a complete thought.
**sen·tence** /sen′təns/ *noun, plural* **sentences.**

**serve** 1. To place food on a table. The waiter *served* us quickly. 2. To be a servant to; do certain duties for; work. The maid *served* the family for many years.
**serve** /sėrv/ *verb,* **served, serving.**

**shadow** A dark area made when rays of light are blocked by a person or thing.
**shad·ow** /shad′ō/ *noun, plural* **shad-ows.**

at; āges; fäther; cär; dãring; end; mē; tėrm; it; tiger; souvenir; hot; ōld; ôff; oil; fôrk; out; up; fůll; trüly; mūsic; sing; thin; zh in treasure; ə in lemon, ago, pencil, taken, circus; ər in letter, honor, dollar.

**shall**   I *shall* be home tomorrow. I *shall* go to the party.
  **shall** /shal/ *verb.*

**shape**   **1.** Form; figure. All circles have the same *shape*. **2.** Condition. He was in bad *shape* after his fall.
  **shape** /shāp/ *noun, plural* **shapes.**

**shark**   A fish that lives in the sea. A shark has gray scales and a large mouth with sharp teeth.
  **shark** /shärk/ *noun, plural* **sharks.**

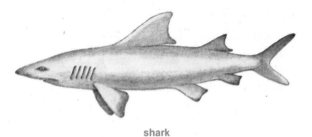

shark

**sheep**   An animal covered with wool that is related to the goat.
  **sheep** /shēp/ *noun, plural* **sheep.**

**she'll**   *She'll* be here tomorrow until noon.
  **she'll** /shēl/ *contraction* for **she will.**

**she's**   *She's* late this morning. *She's* been doing her homework.
  **she's** /shēz/ *contraction* for **she is** and **she has.**

**ship**   **1.** A large boat. **2.** An airplane or spacecraft. **3.** To send by ship, train, truck, or airplane. The factory will *ship* the furniture by truck.
  **ship** /ship/ *noun, plural* **ships;** *verb,* **shipped, shipping.**

**shoe**   An outer covering for the foot. Shoes are usually made of leather.
  **shoe** /shü/ *noun, plural* **shoes.**

**shower**   **1.** A short fall of rain. **2.** A bath in which water is sprayed from overhead. **3.** To bathe by taking a shower.
  **show·er** /shou'ər/ *noun, plural* **showers;** *verb,* **showered, showering.**

**silent**   Completely quiet; still. We crept through the *silent* house.
  **si·lent** /si'lənt/ *adjective.*

**silly**   Without common sense; foolish.
  **sil·ly** /sil'ē/ *adjective,* **sillier, sillient.**

**simile**   A figure of speech in which one object or idea is compared with another in order to suggest that they are alike. For example: *His face shone like the sun. Her hands were as cold as ice.*
  **sim·i·le** /sim'ə lē/ *noun, plural* **similes.**

**since**   John left last week and has been away ever *since. Since* the car isn't working, we'll have to take the bus.
  **since** /sins/ *adverb; preposition.*

**sing**   To make words or sounds with musical tones. The birds *sang* at noon.
  **sing** /sing/ *verb,* **sang** or **sung, sung, singing.**

**sink**   **1.** To go down partly or completely. The wheels of the car *sank* into the mud. **2.** A basin of metal or porcelain that is used for washing. A sink has faucets to turn water on and off and a drain to take water away.
  **sink** /singk/ *verb,* **sank** or **sunk, sunk** or **sunken, sinking;** *noun, plural* **sinks.**

**sir**   A title used in place of a man's name. The sales clerk said to the man, "May I help you, *sir?*"
  **sir** /sėr/ *noun, plural* **sirs.**

**sister**   A girl or woman with the same mother and father as another person.
  **sis·ter** /sis'tər/ *noun, plural* **sisters.**

**six** One more than five; 6

six /siks/ *noun, plural* **sixes;** *adjective.*

**size** 1. The amount of space something takes up; the length, width, and height of something. 2. A series of measurements used for shoes, clothing, and other things sold in stores.

size /sīz/ *noun, plural* **sizes.**

**skate** 1. A special shoe with a metal runner attached to the sole; ice skate. It is used for moving over ice. 2. A skate with small wheels attached to the sole; roller skate. It is used for moving over a flat surface, like a sidewalk. 3. To glide or move along on skates.

skate /skāt/ *noun, plural* **skates;** *verb,* **skated, skating.**

skate

**skeleton** A framework of bones that supports the body of all animals with backbones like birds, fish, and man.

skel·e·ton /skel'ət ən/ *noun, plural* **skeletons.**

**ski** 1. One of a pair of long, narrow runners that curve upward at the front. 2. To travel on skis.

ski /skē/ *noun, plural* **skis** or **ski;** *verb,* **skied, skiing.**

**skip** 1. To spring or bound along, hopping lightly on one foot and then on the other. 2. To pass by or leave out.

skip /skip/ *verb,* **skipped, skipping.**

**skunk** A black animal that has a bushy tail and white stripes along its back. A skunk sprays a strong, bad-smelling liquid when it is frightened or attacked.

skunk /skungk/ *noun, plural* **skunks.**

**sky** The upper space or air beyond the earth. On clear days, the sky has a light-blue color.

sky /skī/ *noun, plural* **skies.**

**skyline** 1. The outline of buildings, mountains, or other objects as seen against the sky. 2. The line at which the earth and sky seem to come together; horizon.

sky·line /skī'līn'/ *noun, plural* **skylines.**

**slippery** Causing or likely to cause slipping or sliding. Freezing rain made the roads *slippery.*

slip·per·y /slip'ər ē/ *adjective,* **slipperier, slipperiest.**

**small** Not large; little.

small /smôl/ *adjective,* **smaller, smallest.**

**smell** 1. To know or become aware of an odor by using the nose. 2. To have or give off an odor that is very often bad. 3. An odor or scent.

smell /smel/ *verb,* **smelled** or **smelt, smelling;** *noun, plural* **smells.**

**smile** 1. An expression of the face that is made by turning up the corners of the mouth. 2. To have or give a smile.

smile /smīl/ *noun, plural* **smiles;** *verb,* **smiled, smiling.**

at; āges; fäther; cär; daring; end; mē; tėrm; it; tīger; souvenir; hot; ōld; ôff; oil; fôrk; out; up; fůll; trūly; mūsic; sing; thin; zh in treasure; ə in lemon, ago, pencil, taken, circus; ər in letter, honor, dollar.

**smoke** **1.** A gas that is given off from something that is burning. **2.** To send out or produce smoke. We could see a chimney *smoking* in the distance. **3.** To draw in and breathe out smoke from tobacco. Dad *smokes* a pipe.
　**smoke** /smōk/ *noun, plural* **smokes;** *verb,* **smoked, smoking.**

**smooth** **1.** Having a surface that is not uneven or rough. **2.** Even or gentle.
　**smooth** /smū<u>th</u>/ *adjective,* **smoother, smoothest.**

**snake** A kind of animal that has a long body covered with scales and no legs, arms, or wings.
　**snake** /snāk/ *noun, plural* **snakes.**

snake

**snap** **1.** To make a sudden, sharp sound. Henry *snapped* his fingers. **2.** To break suddenly and sharply. The twig *snapped* when I stepped on it. **3.** To seize or snatch suddenly or eagerly. The fish *snapped* at the bait. **4.** To take a photograph. Ruth *snapped* a picture of her sister. **5.** A fastener or clasp. Sue replaced the *snap* on her dress.
　**snap** /snap/ *verb,* **snapped, snapping;** *noun, plural* **snaps.**

**snow** **1.** Soft, white crystals or flakes of ice formed by water vapor that freezes in the air. **2.** To fall as snow.
　**snow** /snō/ *noun, plural* **snows;** *verb,* **snowed, snowing.**

**snowfall** A fall of snow. Last night we had our first *snowfall* of winter.
　**snow·fall** /snō'fôl/ *noun, plural* **snowfalls.**

**sold** We *sold* our house last week.
　**sold** /sōld/ *verb.*

**some** *Some* birds cannot fly. *Some* of the girls want to start a softball team.
　**some** /sum/ *adjective; pronoun.*

**something** *Something* is wrong with the car. He looks *something* like me.
　**some·thing** /sum'thing/ *pronoun; adverb.*

**sometime** I saw that movie *sometime* last year.
　**some·time** /sum'tīm'/ *adverb.*

**song** **1.** A piece of music that is sung. **2.** The musical call of a bird.
　**song** /sông/ *noun, plural* **songs.**

**soon** **1.** In a short time. Come to visit us again *soon.* **2.** Early. The guests arrived too *soon,* and we weren't ready **3.** Quickly. I'll be there as *soon* as I can.
　**soon** /sün/ *adverb.*

**sore** **1.** Painful; hurting. Randy's back was *sore* from lifting the boxes. **2.** A place on the body that has been hurt. There was a *sore* on his arm.
　**sore** /sôr/ *adjective,* **sorer, sorest;** *noun, plural* **sores.**

**speech** **1.** The ability to use spoken words to express ideas, thoughts, and feelings. **2.** Something spoken; talk.
　**speech** /spēch/ *noun, plural* **speeches.**

**speed** **1.** Quick or fast motion. Jim ran with great *speed* and won the race. **2.** To move quickly or rapidly. We *sped* down the hill on our sleds.
　**speed** /spēd/ *noun, plural* **speeds;** *verb,* **sped** or **speeded, speeding.**

**spell**  To write or say the letters of a word in the right order.

**spell** /spel/ *verb,* **spelled** or **spelt, spelling.**

**spend**  **1.** To pay out money. Harriet said she could *spend* ten dollars on a scarf. **2.** To pass time. We *spent* the weekend in the country.

**spend** /spend/ *verb,* **spent, spending.**

**sponge**  **1.** A water animal that lives attached to rocks. A sponge has a body that is full of holes and absorbs water easily. **2.** A cleaning pad made to look like the skeleton of a sponge.

**sponge** /spunj/ *noun, plural* **sponges.**

**spoon**  A utensil with a small, shallow bowl at one end of a handle. A spoon is used for eating, measuring, or stirring.

**spoon** /spün/ *noun, plural* **spoons.**

**sport**  **1.** A game in which a person is physically active and often is competing with someone else. Baseball, bowling, swimming, and sailing are kinds of sports. **2.** A person who plays fair and is a good loser. Ann is always a good *sport* when she plays cards.

**sport** /spôrt/ *noun, plural* **sports.**

**spot**  **1.** A mark or stain left by dirt, food, or other matter. **2.** A mark or part on something that is different from the rest. My dog is white with black *spots*. **3.** A place. That park is a pleasant *spot* for a picnic. **4.** To mark or be marked with a stain or blot. The paint *spotted* the floor. **5.** To see; recognize. I *spotted* Susan in the crowd.

**spot** /spot/ *noun, plural* **spots;** *verb,* **spotted, spotting.**

**spring**  **1.** To move forward or jump up quickly; leap. She had to *spring* out of the way to avoid being hit by the car. **2.** A jump or leap. The acrobat made a beautiful *spring* from one trapeze to the next. **3.** The season of the year that comes between winter and summer.

**spring** /spring/ *verb,* **sprang** or **sprung, sprung, springing;** .*noun, plural* **springs.**

**squirrel**  A small, furry animal with a long, bushy tail seen in and around trees. It is a member of the rodent family.

**squir·rel** /skwėr′əl/ *noun, plural* **squir- rels.**

squirrel

**stake**  A stick or post pointed at one end so that it can be driven into the ground. The campers drove *stakes* into the ground and tied the corners of the tent to them.

**stake** /stāk/ *noun, plural* **stakes.**

**star**  A heavenly body that looks like a bright point of light in the night sky.

**star** /stär/ *noun, plural* **stars.**

**start**  To begin something.

**start** /stärt/ *verb,* **started, starting.**

at; āges; fäther; cär; dãring; end; mē; tėrm; it; tīger; souvenir; hot; ōld; ôff; oil; fôrk; out; up; fúll; trūly; mūsic; sing; thin; zh in treasure; ə in lemon, ago, pencil, taken, circus; ər in letter, honor, dollar.

**state**  1. A group of people living together under one government. 2. To show or explain in words. Can you *state* your name and phone number?
  **state** /stāt/ *noun, plural* **states;** *verb,* **stated, stating.**

**statue**  A likeness of a person or animal that is made out of stone, bronze, clay, or some other solid material.
  **stat·ue** /stach′ü/ *noun, plural* **statues.**

**stay**  To wait in one place.
  **stay** /stā/ *verb,* **stayed, staying.**

**steak**  A slice of meat or fish for broiling or frying.
  **steak** /stāk/ *noun, plural* **steaks.**

**steal**  1. To take something that does not belong to one. 2. To get to the next base in baseball without advancing by a hit or error.
  **steal** /stēl/ *verb,* **stole, stolen, stealing.**

**steam**  Water in the form of a gas or vapor. Water gives off steam when it is heated to the boiling point.
  **steam** /stēm/ *noun.*

steam

**step**  1. The movement of lifting the foot and putting it down again in a new place. 2. A stair or rung of a ladder. 3. To move by taking a step or steps.
  **step** /step/ *noun, plural* **steps,** *verb,* **stepped, stepping.**

**stew**  A dish made of pieces of meat or fish and vegetables cooked together in a liquid. We had beef *stew* for dinner.
  **stew** /stü/ *or* /stū/ *noun, plural* **stews.**

**stick**  1. A long thin piece of wood. 2. To make something stay on or attach. *Stick* a stamp on the envelope.
  **stick** /stik/ *noun, plural* **sticks;** *verb,* **stuck, sticking.**

**stir**  1. To mix something by moving it around in a circular motion with a spoon, stick, or similar object. 2. To move or cause to move about.
  **stir** /stėr/ *verb,* **stirred, stirring.**

**stone**  The hard material that rocks are made of.
  **stone** /stōn/ *noun, plural* **stones.**

**stop**  1. To keep from moving or doing something. The driver tried to *stop* the car. 2. A place where a stop is made. The bus *stop* is at the corner.
  **stop** /stop/ *verb,* **stopped, stopping;** *noun, plural* **stops.**

**store**  A place where goods are sold.
  **store** /stôr/ *noun, plural* **stores.**

**storm**  A strong wind with heavy rain, hail, sleet, or snow.
  **storm** /stôrm/ *noun, plural* **storms.**

**stove**  A large object made of metal, used for cooking or heating.
  **stove** /stōv/ *noun, plural* **stoves.**

**stranger**  A person whom one does not know. I was a *stranger* in that place.
  **stran·ger** /strān′jər/ *noun, plural* **strangers.**

**study**  To try to learn by reading or thinking about something. Our class *studied* the planets of the solar system.
  **stud·y** /stud′ē/ *verb,* **studied, studying.**

**subject**   A word or group of words that does the action of the verb in a sentence.
**sub·ject** /sub′jikt/ *noun, plural* **subjects.**

**subtract**   To take away from. If you *subtract* 3 from 7, you have 4.
**sub·tract** /səb trakt′/ *verb,* **subtracted, subtracting**

**sudden**   **1.** Happening without warning. A *sudden* snowstorm trapped many cars on the highway. **2.** Quick. He made a *sudden* decision.
**sud·den** /sud′ən/ *adjective.*

**summer**   The season of the year that comes between spring and autumn.
**sum·mer** /sum′ər/ *noun, plural* **summers.**

**Sunday**   The first day of the week.
**Sun·day** /sun′dē/ *or* /sun′dā/ *noun, plural* **Sundays.**

**sung**   The choir has *sung* many songs.
**sung** /sung/ *verb.*

**sunny**   Full of sunlight. It is a *sunny* day today.
**sun·ny** /sun′ē/ *adjective,* **sunnier, sunniest.**

**sunset**   The setting of the sun at the end of the day.
**sun·set** /sun′set′/ *noun, plural* **sunsets.**

**suppose**   **1.** To believe. I *suppose* that I'll be finished with my homework soon. **2.** To expect or require. She is *supposed* to be here now.
**sup·pose** /sə pōz′/ *verb,* **supposed, supposing.**

**sure**   **1.** Having no doubt. He is *sure* that he is right **2.** Certain to be. Our team is a *sure* winner.
**sure** /shu̇r/ *adjective,* **surer, surest.**

**surprise**   A feeling of wonder or amazement caused by something unexpected.
**sur·prise** /sər prīz′/ *noun, plural* **surprises.**

**sweep**   To clean with a broom or brush.
**sweep** /swēp/ *verb,* **swept, sweeping.**

**swim**   To move in the water by using arms or legs, or fins and tail.
**swim** /swim/ *verb,* **swam, swum, swimming.**

**swing**   **1.** To move back and forth with a steady motion. Bill likes to *swing* on an old tire that hangs by a rope from a tree. **2.** A seat hung by chains or ropes in which a person can sit and swing. We enjoy the *swings* in playground.
**swing** /swing/ *verb,* **swung, swinging;** *noun, plural* **swings.**

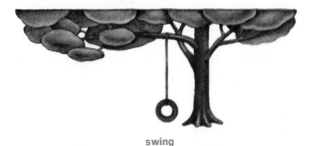
swing

**symbol**   Something that stands for or represents something else. The dove is a *symbol* of peace. The mark **+** is the *symbol* for addition.
**sym·bol** /sim′bəl/ *noun, plural* **symbols.**

at; āges; fäther; cär; dâring; end; mē; tėrm; it; tīger; souvenir; hot; ōld; ôff; oil; fôrk; out; up; fu̇ll; trüly; mūsic; sing; thin; zh in treasure; ə in lemon, ago, pencil, taken, circus; ər in letter, honor, dollar.

**T**

**tail**  The part of an animal's body that sticks out from the back end.
**tail** /tāl/ *noun, plural* **tails.**

tail

**tall**  Not short or low. That building is *tall*. Giraffes are the *tallest* animals.
**tall** /tôl/ *adjective,* **taller, tallest.**

**tax**  Money that people must pay for the support of the government.
**tax** /taks/ *noun, plural* **taxes.**

**teacher**  A person who gives lessons or classes. My father is an English *teacher*.
**teach·er** /tē′chər/ *noun, plural* **teachers.**

**team**  A group that plays or acts together. Our school has a soccer *team*.
**team** /tēm/ *noun, plural* **teams.**

**tear**  1. To pull or become pulled apart. I *tore* a hole in my coat. 2. A torn part or place. The tailor sewed the *tear* in my coat. The old flag was *torn* to shreds.
**tear** /târ/ *verb,* **tore, torn, tearing;** *noun, plural* **tears.**

**than**  A cow is bigger *than* a rabbit.
**than** /than/ *or* /thən/ *conjunction.*

**thank**  To say that one is pleased or grateful. *Thank* you for your help.
**thank** /thangk/ *verb,* **thanked, thanking.**

**Thanksgiving**  A holiday celebrated as a day of thanksgiving and feasting. It falls on the fourth Thursday in November in the United States.
**Thanks·giv·ing** /thangks′giv′ing/ *noun, plural* **Thanksgivings.**

**that**  *That* girl won the prize. I prefer this dress to *that*. The boy *that* lives next door is in my class at school. He stayed up so late *that* he was tired the next day.
**that** /that/ *adjective; pronoun, plural* **those;** *conjunction; adverb.*

**that's**  *That's* the book I lost.
**that's** /thats/ *contraction* for **that is.**

**them**  Rick surprised his parents by giving *them* a gift.
**them** /them/ *or* /thəm/ *pronoun.*

**then**  The play ended and *then* the curtain went down. I hope we will finish the work before *then*.
**then** /then/ *adverb; noun.*

**there's**  *There's* my friend, Ann.
**there's** /thârz/ *contraction* for **there is.**

**they**  *They* like to sing together.
**they** /thā/ *pronoun plural.*

**they're**  *They're* going to England.
**they're** /thâr/ *contraction* for **they are.**

**thing**  1. Whatever is spoken of, thought of, or done. That was an unkind *thing* to say. 2. Something that can be touched, seen, heard, smelled, or tasted but is not alive. A book is a *thing*.
**thing** /thing/ *noun, plural* **things.**

**think**  1. To use the mind to form ideas or to make decisions. *Think* it over carefully before you give me your final answer. 2. To have an opinion, belief, or idea. She *thought* we were sisters.
**think** /thingk/ *verb,* **thought, thinking.**

**third**  1. Next after the second. 2. One of three equal parts, ⅓.

**third** /thėrd/ *adjective; noun, plural* **thirds.**

**thirst** The desire or need for something to drink. Water satisfied my *thirst*.
**thirst** /thėrst/ *noun, plural* **thirsts.**

**thirsty** Lacking water or moisture. The girls were *thirsty* after the long hike.
**thirst·y** /thėrs'tē/ *adjective,* **thirstier, thirstiest.**

**thirty** 30.
**thir·ty** /thėr'tē/ *noun, plural* **thirties;** *adjective.*

**thought** 1. I *thought* Dad was going to take us to the zoo this afternoon. 2. Ideas or opinions. What are your *thoughts* on how to solve this problem?
**thought** /thôt/ *verb; noun, plural* **thoughts.**

**three** One more than two; 3.
**three** /thrē/ *noun, plural* **threes;** *adjective.*

**thumb** The short, thick finger on the hand.
**thumb** /thum/ *noun, plural* **thumbs.**

**Thursday** The fifth day of the week.
**Thurs·day** /thėrz'dē/ *or* /thėrz'dā/ *noun, plural* **Thursdays.**

**tiger** A large striped animal that is a member of the cat family.
**ti·ger** /tī'gər/ *noun, plural* **tigers.**

**time** 1. The period during which events or actions happen or continue. Dinosaurs lived a long *time* ago. 2. An exact point in time. What *time* is it?
**time** /tīm/ *noun, plural* **times.**

**tired** Worn-out. Ruth was *tired* after playing tennis for an hour.
**tired** /tīrd/ *adjective.*

**tissue** A soft, thin paper that easily absorbs moisture.
**tis·sue** /tish'ü/ *noun, plural* **tissues.**

**to** Joan gave the letter *to* her sister.
**to** /tü/ *preposition*

**toad** An animal that is like a frog.
**toad** /tōd/ *noun, plural* **toads.**

toad

**toast** 1. Sliced bread that has been browned by heat. 2. To brown by heating. We *toasted* bread by the fire.
**toast** /tōst/ *noun; verb,* **toasted, toasting.**

**today** The present time or present day.
**to·day** /tə dā'/ *noun.*

**together** With one another.
**to·geth·er** /tə geth'ər/ *adverb.*

**told** Jane *told* me a secret.
**told** /tōld/ *verb.*

**tomorrow** The day after today.
**to·mor·row** /tə môr'ō/ *or* /tə mor'ō/ *noun.*

**tonight** The night of this day.
**to·night** /tə nīt'/ *noun.*

**too** There are *too* many people for one car. May we go, *too?*
**too** /tü/ *adverb.*

at; āges; fäther; cär; dàring; end; mē; tėrm; it; tīger; souvenir; hot; ōld; ôff; oil; fôrk; out; up; fůll; trüly; mūsic; sing; thin; zh in treasure; ə in lemon, ago, pencil, taken, circus; ər in letter, honor, dollar.

**toy** Something for a child to play with.
**toy** /toi/ *noun, plural* **toys.**

toys

**trade** 1. The giving of one thing in exchange for something else. I made a *trade* of my apple for her orange. 2. To give one thing in exchange for something else. I *traded* four of my baseball cards for three of his.
**trade** /trād/ *noun, plural* **trades.**

**train** A line of railroad cars connected together. Some trains carry passengers; other trains carry only freight.
**train** /trān/ *noun, plural* **trains.**

**travel** To go from one place to another.
**trav·el** /trav'əl/ *verb,* **traveled, traveling.**

**tree** A plant with a woody trunk with branches and leaves.
**tree** /trē/ *noun, plural* **trees.**

**trip** 1. The act of traveling or going from one place to another. 2. To catch one's foot on something and stumble or fall. He *tripped* on the edge of the rug.
**trip** /trip/ *noun, plural* **trips;** *verb,* **tripped, tripping.**

**trouble** 1. A difficult or dangerous situation. The people in the valley will be in *trouble* if the dam breaks. 2. Extra work or effort. Jane went to a lot of *trouble* to make this dinner a success.
**trou·ble** /trub'əl/ *noun, plural* **trouble.**

**truck** A large motor vehicle that is made to carry heavy loads.
**truck** /truk/ *noun, plural* **trucks.**

**try** To make an effort to do something. Please *try* not to be late.
**try** /trī/ *verb,* **tried, trying.**

**Tuesday** The third day of the week.
**Tues·day** /tüz'dē/ *or* /tūz'dā/ *noun, plural* **Tuesdays.**

**tune** A series of notes that make up a song or the melody of a piece of music.
**tune** /tün/ *or* /tūn/ *noun, plural* **tunes.**

**tunnel** A long passage built underneath the ground or water. There is a subway *tunnel* under the river.
**tun·nel** /tun'əl/ *noun, plural* **tunnels.**

**turkey** A large bird that is raised as food, especially for Thanksgiving.
**tur·key** /tėr'kē/ *noun, plural* **turkeys.**

**turn** 1. To go or make go a certain or different way. Pam *turned* the car left at the corner. 2. A change in position or direction. There is a sharp *turn* in the road. 3. A time, occasion, or chance at something. It's Mike's *turn* at bat.
**turn** /tėrn/ *verb,* **turned, turning;** *noun, plural* **turns.**

**twice** Two times.
**twice** /twīs/ *adverb.*

**two** One more than one; a pair of; 2.
**two** /tü/ *noun, plural* **twos;** *adjective.*

## U

**uncle** 1. The brother of one's mother or father. 2. The husband of one's aunt.
**un·cle** /ung'kəl/ *noun, plural* **uncles.**

**under** The kitten crawled *under* the sofa. The damaged boat slowly sank *under* water. Jeff scooped mud off the *under* part of his shoe.
**un·der** /un'dər/ *preposition; adverb; adjective.*

**until**   Wait *until* eight o'clock.
**un·til** /ən til´/ *or* /un til´/ *preposition.*

**up**   We looked *up* to see the airplane. Food prices were *up* again this month. The spider climbed *up* the wall.
**up** /up/ *adverb; adjective; preposition.*

**us**   We called him, but he didn't see *us*.
**us** /us/ *or* /əs/ *pronoun.*

**use**   **1.** To put into service for a particular purpose. May I *use* your scissors? **2.** To finish completely. We *used* up all the butter at breakfast. **3.** The act of using or the state of being used. Tom made the bookcase with the *use* of a saw and a hammer and nails. **4.** A need or purpose for which something is used. Do you have any *use* for empty bottles?
**use** /ūz/ *for verb;* /ūs/ *for noun; verb,* **used, using;** *noun, plural* **uses.**

**useful**   Helpful. A pocketknife can be very *useful* on a camping trip.
**use·ful** /ūs fəl/ *adjective.*

**usual**   Common or expected. Hot weather is *usual* for July and August.
**u·su·al** /ū´zhü əl/ *adjective.*

### V

**vacation**   A period of rest or freedom from school, business, or other activity.
**va·ca·tion** /vā kā´shən/ *noun, plural* **vacations.**

**valley**   An area of low land between hills or mountains. Valleys often have rivers flowing through them.
**val·ley** /val´ē/ *noun, plural* **valleys.**

**verb**   A word that expresses action or state of being. *Run, think, buy, go,* and *be* are verbs.
**verb** /vėrb/ *noun, plural* **verbs.**

**very**   That boy is *very* strong for his age. That actor is at the *very* top of his career.
**ver·y** /ver´ē/ *adverb.*

**village**   A small group of houses. A village is usually smaller than a town.
**vil·lage** /vil´ij/ *noun, plural* **villages.**

**vowel**   A voiced speech sound made by not blocking the flow of air through the mouth. **A, e, i, o, u,** and sometimes **y** are the letters with such a sound.
**vow·el** /vou´əl/ *noun, plural* **vowels.**

### W

**wagon**   **1.** A vehicle that has four wheels, for example, station *wagon*. **2.** A child's low, four-wheeled vehicle.
**wag·on** /wag´ən/ *noun, plural* **wagons.**

wagon

**wait**   To stay in a place until someone comes or something happens. *Wait* until it stops raining before you leave.
**wait** /wāt/ *verb,* **waited, waiting.**

**wake**   **1.** To stop sleeping. What time did you *wake* up this morning. **2.** To stop from sleeping. Be quiet or you will *wake* the baby.
**wake** /wāk/ *verb,* **waked** or **woke, waked, waking.**

at; āges; fäther; cär; dãring; end; mē; tėrm; it; tīger; souvenir; hot; ōld; ôff; oil; fôrk; out; up; fûll; trüly; mūsic; sing; thin; zh in treasure; ə in lemon, ago, pencil, taken, circus; ər in letter, honor, dollar.

**wall**   A structure made of stone, plaster, wood, brick, or other material. Walls form the sides of buildings or rooms.
**wall** /wôl/ *noun, plural* **walls.**

**want**   To have a wish for.
**want** /wont/ *or* /wônt/ *verb,* **wanted, wanting.**

**was**   I *was* at home yesterday.
**was** /wuz/ *or* /woz/ *or* /wəz/ *verb.*

**weak**   Not having strength, force, or power. Lack of food made the hikers *weak.*
**weak** /wēk/ *adjective,* **weaker, weakest.**

**wear**   To carry or have on the body. We *wear* warm clothes in the winter.
**wear** /wār/ *verb,* **wore, worn, wearing.**

**Wednesday**   The fourth day.
**Wednes·day** /wenz′dē/ *or* /wenz′dā/ *noun, plural* **Wednesdays.**

**weed**   A plant that is useless or harmful and grows where it is not wanted. We pulled the *weeds* out of our garden.
**weed** /wēd/ *noun, plural* **weeds.**

**week**   A period of seven days.
**week** /wēk/ *noun, plural* **weeks.**

**well**   **1.** In a good way. Ann plays soccer *well.* **2.** In good health. I feel *well* today. **3.** A hole or pit made in the ground to get water, oil, or gas.
**well** /wel/ *adverb; adjective,* **better, best;** *noun, plural* **wells.**

**went**   I *went* to bed early last night.
**went** /went/ *verb.*

**were**   We *were* at home all day.
**were** /wėr/ *verb.*

**we're**   *We're* going home now.
**we're** /wir/ *contraction* for **we are.**

**whale**   A large animal that has a body like a fish.

**whale** /hwāl/ *noun, plural* **whales** or **whale.**

**what's**   *What's* his name? *What's* happened? *What's* she done?
**what's** /hwuts/ *or* /hwots/ *contraction* for **what is** and **what has.**

**when**   *When* did you get to school? The children played until noon, *when* they had lunch. Since *when* have you liked to take long walks?
**when** /hwen/ *adverb; conjunction; pronoun.*

**where**   *Where* does he live? The keys are still *where* you left them last night.
**where** /hwâr/ *adverb; conjunction.*

**which**   *Which* of the books did you like best? *Which* girl is your sister?
**which** /hwich/ *pronoun; adjective.*

**while**   We stopped and rested for a *while.* Did anyone call *while* I was away?
**while** /hwīl/ *noun; conjunction.*

**white**   The lightest of all colors; the opposite of black. White is the color of fresh snow, milk, and polar bears.
**white** /hwīt/ *adjective,* **whiter, whitest.**

**whole**   Having all its parts. Have you read the *whole* book already?
**whole** /hōl/ *adjective.*

**wild**   Not controlled by people; living or growing naturally. *Wild* flowers grew along the road.
**wild** /wīld/ *adjective;* **wilder, wildest.**

wild

**will**   She *will* visit you tonight.
**will** /wil/ *verb.*

**wish**   To want something very much. Ruth *wished* she had a kitten.
  **wish** /wish/ *verb*, **wished, wishing.**

**with**   We went to the circus *with* our friends. What goes *with* chicken?
  **with** /wi<u>th</u>/ *or* /with/ *preposition.*

**woman**   An adult female person.
  **wom·an** /wům′ən/ *noun, plural* **women.**

**women**   More than one woman.
  **wom·en** /wim′ən/ *noun plural.*

**won**   Who *won* the first prize?
  **won** /wun/ *verb.*

**won't**   He *won't* be able to finish the work today. They *won't* know how.
  **won't** /wōnt/ *contraction* for **will not.**

**wood**   The hard material that makes up the trunk and branches of a tree or bush.
  **wood** /wůd/ *noun, plural* **woods.**

**woodlands**   Land covered with woods.
  **wood·lands** /wůd′ləndz/ *noun, plural.*

**woolen**   Made of wool.
  **wool·en** /wůl′ən/ *adjective.*

**wrap**   To fold or put a cover around someone or something. Ruth enjoys *wrapping* presents.
  **wrap** /rap/ *verb*, **wrapped** or **wrapt, wrapping.**

**wren**   A songbird.
  **wren** /ren/ *noun, plural* **wrens.**

**wrinkle**   A small fold, ridge, or line in a smooth surface. Mary ironed the *wrinkles* out of her dress.
  **wrin·kle** /ring′kəl/ *noun, plural* **wrinkles.**

**write**   1. To form the letters, words, or symbols of something on paper or some other surface. 2. To make up stories, poems. 3. To send a letter.
  **write** /rīt/ *verb*, **wrote, written, writing.**

**writing**   1. Letters, words, or symbols that are written by hand. Her *writing* is neat and easy to read. 2. A book, play, or other thing that has been written.
  **writ·ing** /rī′ting/ *noun, plural* **writings.**

**written**   Joan has *written* her report.
  **writ·ten** /rit′ən/ *verb.*

**wrong**   1. Not correct or true. Her answer to the question was *wrong.* 2. Not moral or good; bad. It was *wrong* of him to steal. 3. Not proper. A heavy sweater is the *wrong* thing to wear on a hot day.
  **wrong** /rông/ *adjective.*

**wrote**   He *wrote* down what she said.
  **wrote** /rōt/ *verb.*

## Y

**yellow**   1. The color of gold, butter, or ripe lemons. 2. Having the color yellow.
  **yel·low** /yel′ō/ *noun, plural* **yellows;** *adjective,* **yellower, yellowest;** *verb,* **yellowed, yellowing.**

**yes**   *Yes,* you are right.
  **yes** /yes/ *noun, plural* **yeses.**

**you've**   *You've* got to do better than that.
  **you've** /yův/ *contraction* for **you have.**

## Z

**zoo**   A park or other place where animals are kept for exhibition.
  **zoo** /zü/ *noun, plural* **zoos.**

---

at; āges; fäther; cär; dāring; end; mē; tèrm; it; tīger; souvenir; hot; ōld; ôff; oil; fôrk; out; up; fůll; trüly; mūsic; sing; thin; zh in treasure; ə in lemon, ago, pencil, taken, circus; ər in letter, honor, dollar.

# HANDWRITING MODELS

a b c d e f g
h i j k l m n
o p q r s t u
v w x y z

A B C D E F G
H I J K L M N
O P Q R S T U
V W X Y Z